I'LL RAISE YOU TEN

W9-BRG-717

I'LL RAISE YOU TEN *by*

Denise O'Donnell Adams
A Memoir

gatekeeper press™
Columbus, Ohio

The views and opinions expressed in this book are solely those of the author and do not reflect the views or opinions of Gatekeeper Press. Gatekeeper Press is not to be held responsible for and expressly disclaims responsibility of the content herein.

I'll Raise You Ten

The stories in this book reflect the author's recollection of events. Some names, dates, locations and identifying characteristics have been changed to protect the privacy of those depicted. Dialogue has been re-created from memory.

Published by Gatekeeper Press
2167 Stringtown Rd, Suite 109
Columbus, OH 43123-2989
www.GatekeeperPress.com

Copyright © 2020 by Denise O'Donnell Adams
All rights reserved. Neither this book, nor any parts within it may be sold or reproduced in any form or by any electronic or mechanical means, including information storage and retrieval systems, without permission in writing from the author. The only exception is by a reviewer, who may quote short excerpts in a review.

ISBN (paperback): 9781662904219

CONTENTS

DEDICATION

Without question, my story should be dedicated to one and only one person alone... my savior, friend, second mother, and teacher, Aunt Edna. Without her unconditional love for her younger sister and the ten of us, this book would not have been written. Any good, any knowledge, anything that keeps me sane, grounded, and full of love and hope has been a direct result of having her in my life and the lives of the O'Donnell children. You are greatly missed every day of my life... Thank you, God, for sharing this saint with those who needed saving. Abundant love to you, Aunt Edna...

Your niece,
—Denise

FOREWORD

"Life is only bearable when the mind and body are in harmony, and there is a natural balance between them, and each other has a natural respect for the other."

—D. H. Lawrence.

I've always wondered if Mom saw herself as a prisoner and we were the rats running around her cell. I suppose that would make Dad her cellmate. God was their warden... What were their crimes and how long was their sentence? Their addictions were their crimes. Their sentence was a lifetime.

Why am I writing this book? That's a very good question. I was discussing the many reasons why with my sister Lisa and husband David. I was coming up blank. It took me several weeks to finally articulate the importance of sharing our lives with the masses. We need to be heard; we need validation. Protecting our abusers has crippled the ten of us in a myriad of ways. The list of disorders we have been carrying around with us for the past five decades is endless.

I'm writing this book because there has always been a pain in my heart and a voice in my head saying, "Don't let them get away with it." I hope that my honesty will possibly help other abusers as well as the abused wake up and see what tragic effects hurting and silence demand. It's difficult for us to tolerate outside praises about either us or our parents. We don't care about any of that. If only they could read our minds while we are smiling and nodding, pretending that it's all true.

If someone throws a hundred compliments your way but sneaks in just one little insult, human nature predicts that we will focus on the insult, regardless. Our lives were one big insult, lacking any compliments from the two that mattered. How about "I love you"? That would have been refreshing. We did have some good times. There was a bit of fun every now and then. The problem was that the good times were not enough to outweigh the bad, and certainly not enough to heal our souls. We are all still working on that. It's most definitely a work in progress for the ten of us, although sadly, a few of us haven't even begun!

It takes something out of you, pretending. You never get it back. The drain is exhausting, yet you go on. You look in the mirror and even then you trick yourself into believing you are someone else, someone who is loved, appreciated, missed.

It is fleeting, so you return and start all over. The days turn into weeks, then months, then years and the only change is an older face staring back. It's become a way of life, your life. Your true self was stolen. And the sad part is, you know it. It follows you to your grave. Then it is over; the peace has finally arrived.

Please don't be a pretender; it will destroy your life.

—Denise O'Donnell Adams.

AUTHOR'S FOOTNOTE

Throughout my manuscript, I've taken the liberty of including many of my siblings in general agreement of thought, feeling, and emotion. Obviously the remaining nine may not feel the same concerning every scenario written. While my book is a clear, truthful account of my life, it's not a license for inclusion of my sisters' and brothers' feelings. It would be impossible for the ten of us to feel the same, especially with the span of seventeen years between us. Sharing the same parents does allow the ten to relate, understand, and have honest feelings of empathy that bonds us together in ways that only we can perceive. Unconditional love has always been our unequivocal thread that binds us together...

Forever in my love,
—Denise

CHAPTER 1

Black and White

rama began in my life the second I was born. When you only weigh 2 pounds and 11 ounces at birth, this is to be expected. I was born three months early, not a swift move back in 1957. I began my fight for life at our small Catholic hospital of St. Mary's, where all good Catholic girls belong.

Violence was always in my life, from the time I can remember. I remember my sister Theresa lay under the black-and-white leather chair, holding onto the chair legs once again. It seemed like I was surrounded by black and white; the entire decor screamed of it. The only thing that was not black and white was my life, my reality. Even back then nothing made sense. I was using the reasoning of a 3-year-old. The crouching tiger under the living room chair was 5.

I can remember thinking to myself, "What is wrong with her? Why is she so bad? She knows she will be punished by that big man we call Daddy, and yet she acts like a wild animal every chance she gets. Could she possibly *enjoy* being sent under the chair? I am starting to think the answer is yes."

Our green eyes locked on each other. Is she trying to tell me something? He is not paying attention anymore. His eyes are fixed on the square machine across from Theresa's weekly prison. When the big man is here, the machine echoes sports and news religiously.

The address was 423 North Sixth Street, DeKalb, Illinois. This is where I began my memories. Memories that were sometimes nightmares and sometimes fun. More fun would have been my vote and I am sure my nine siblings would agree, but sadly no one was asking us to vote! The only people to show up at the polls were the grown-ups in charge, Richard and Connie—both Democrats in politics, but there was no democracy on Sixth and Fisk taking place during the '50s or beyond.

Nine of us were born while living on Sixth Street, and the last child arrived while we were living above the tavern—"The 1009" (ten-oh-nine) to be exact. The sign above the tavern door actually said "Dick's 1009 Tavern." Our father's name was John Richard O'Donnell, and where the man goes so the nickname will follow. Yes, Dad was a bookie and a tavern owner. The bookie gig came first and lasted a lifetime.

☩　☩　☩

If you are a friend, family member, or one of my father's siblings, I imagine you are a bit upset and shocked after what you've just read. Please do not let the above paragraphs stop you from turning the pages and coming face to face with what the ten of us lived through and how we continued to have hope and faith amid the daily chaos we called home. Yes, the account of the O'Donnells may be difficult to read, but soon you will get an insight into just how difficult it was to live.

Little Richard was singing about Lucille while Elvis was building a mansion in Memphis when I popped onto the scene. My father shared a name with the undisputed "Queen" of rock and roll, and Connie Jean may have been the most loyal fan of the "King," but that's where all similarities ended.

Looking at my birth certificate opened my eyes to a few pieces of the puzzle. Mom was 22 years old and had already buried her first-born son, John Richard Jr. Dad was 30 years old when I was born and had become aware that life could be challenging.

The house across from St. Mary's Church was where my sister Theresa had been waiting patiently for her new baby sibling. Staying in ICU for three months was my saving grace. The valentine month welcomed me into life with Richard, Connie, and big sis Theresa. The miscarriage between Theresa and myself was the reason we were two years apart.

The reason Theresa didn't like me was obvious: jealousy. So why or how could a tiny child of 2 years old be jealous of anyone, especially a newborn? Well, Theresa was used to Mom all to herself for the first year of her young life. She was not happy when Dad returned home from the service, and equally unhappy when I arrived in my bassinet.

Theresa decided she wanted all the attention in the household. She chose the wrong family to become the eldest—and the neediest. Soon she would have to share the attention with a lot more than one sibling... If only she had been aware of the numbers to follow, she may have given up. There would be many faces shared for her to corral.

It was time to make a life-altering decision. Looking across the table, she could clearly see the objects of her affection. They were parents, the major object being the father, the farmer, the bartender, the bookie. She was going to win him over if she had to die trying. This she nearly accomplished many times during her teen years. I used to kid about the paramedics knowing Theresa's social security number while she was in high school. They were at our house often, saving her from herself time and time again! The more pain she caused, the more attention she received. It was no matter to her if most of the pain was directed at herself. This was an innate lesson she learned very quickly in life. Unfortunately, she has continued to revisit this caustic pot of manipulation for decades. Way too late and several husbands and calamities later, the diagnosis of bipolar disorder finally reached Theresa's ears, heart, mind, and soul. No one was surprised and things finally made a bit of sense to the masses.

If I've learned anything from reading detective books and watching television for decades, it's that you can easily figure out the man by going back in time. As Joe Kenda says, "My, my, my." My parents are no exception to the rule. Will this line of thinking hold true for Dick and Connie O'Donnell? Only time will tell. The bigger question is... what price did the twelve of us pay because Dad's chosen profession was that of a gambler and an undercover bookie? What price did we pay because Connie Jean had her own baggage and distorted agenda? Let's begin with Mom.

The graduation festivities in Fulton, Missouri, began and ended in the year 1952 without an appearance from one Constance Jean George. Connie decided, against her parents' wishes, to quit high school and head north to the small farming community of DeKalb, Illinois—home of the Barbed-Wire Barons and Northern Illinois University. The Greyhound may have been slow-moving, but Mom was quick and made no haste finding her two older sisters, Doris and Edna, who had been calling DeKalb home for the past few years.

The spunky teenager hit the streets and headed out with her tiny suitcase to the upstairs apartment in downtown DeKalb for a short pit stop before her life was to begin...

Enter John Richard O'Donnell. Like I said, Mom was in a dash to get things started.

CHAPTER 2

Friendly Tap

Sometimes you want to go where everybody knows your name. The Friendly Tap fit that bill. It was where the action was in downtown DeKalb in the fifties, if you liked to drink and gamble that is. The tavern was tucked in between the DeKalb movie theater and an insurance company on a tiny side-street off the main drag. It wasn't a classy joint, and it did not resemble the infamous bars that the West Side of Chicago was so proud of, but then again, the newly appointed Chicago crime boss, Paul Ricca, and his boys were happy to hang out at the "Green Mill." They didn't need to cross the river into the west suburbs; they had enough runners doing their dirty work in grand style. One of those stylish workers was my very own father, more on that later.

The place was long and narrow, with typical round tables and booths sprinkled tightly throughout. The bar was straight and had the ever-present "Nation" cash register front and center to ring up the sales. That salesman was my father. His fate had been sealed; he was now a barkeep.

Danny hired him on the spot. Danny was a smart guy. Did Dad come right out and say that he liked to gamble? Or that he would love Danny to teach him his given trade? His trade of course was that of a "wise guy." We don't exactly know the answer. Maybe gamblers have a gambler radar, a gamdar! Oh my goodness, I've created a new word for the bookies of America.

The combination of good looks along with his artistic story-telling proved to be a huge asset to Dad. The bar was his stage. He was in his element and it showed. The women liked to sit at the bar and stare at him. The men loved his stories. It was a win-win for all who crossed the threshold at the "Tap."

Mom used to tell the story of how she felt an eerie calmness the exact second she laid eyes on Dad racing behind the bar on that infamous Saturday night in 1953. Of course, it was Dad's extreme Irish good looks that sparked Mom's interest in the beginning. However, beginnings are short-lived, and soon Mom was into the center of the only romance she would ever know.

CHAPTER 3

Becoming a Bookie/and Mom

How long was Dad just a bartender for Danny Kovich before he got his wings to fly? How long until he was deemed a "bookie"? Since my dad never actually admitted to any of us girls that he was a bookie, we have to rely on hearsay. We have heard that Danny taught him everything he ever knew about gambling and the dance of becoming a "sharp" and having a "store." Was it in the cards that Dad would soon leave the tutelage of his Slavic boss and teacher, or was there something or someone lurking in the shadows to catapult Richard over to 1009 and Market?

It was a busy night. Dad was running up and down the bar alley trying to keep up. Friday nights were always crazy. Connie Jean walked in, and the rest is history. She was easy to notice, petite in all the right places, dark wavy hair, strong features with a strong personality to match. Dad was already working alongside two of the George sisters from Missouri. If she wanted to see her older sisters, she had to become a barfly.

Lucky for her, Danny was okay with her borrowing the bar stool. At first, she unnerved Dad, sitting there staring. Sure, he was used to the glares, but something about this filly was different. Mom was only 18 years old. Maybe that was the main reason Dad was feeling uneasy. She was too young for the big man on campus who was nearing 26. She was awful pretty though. Dad liked the way she moved. She was light on her feet, like a dancer. And looking like the movie star Heddy Lamarr did not hurt. They shared the same strikingly dark looks, and both had fame on their minds. Heady wanted worldwide fame. Mom just wanted Dad.

Connie didn't waste any time finding a job or a fiancé. She had both before the full moon rose on her first night in town. If the truth were known, she had both within her first hour in town. The job was a matter of record. The nuptials she was keeping to herself, and from the groom. She would let Richard know when to get fitted for his tux soon enough. There wasn't much reason in getting the man too excited or nervous before the big day.

If Dad would have known what she was thinking within minutes after their first encounter, he might have jumped over the bar counter and run for the fields... or maybe just down the street to Andy's Tap. He could only count diamonds, spades, clubs, and hearts. He left the mind-reading to Mom.

Connie was on the most important mission of her life. How was she going to make Richard notice her and at the same time make him forget about all the other women chasing after him? Mom had been asking around. Even sisters Doris and Edna tried to steer her away from their coworker. Dad was 25 years old and not looking for a serious relationship with an 18-year-old child from Missouri. But Mom had a plan... get the man talking.

Most days, Connie would come into work just a little early—not too early to alert Richard, but early enough to sit on the other side of the bar and learn about Dad, his family, and his passions in life. She learned that Dad was one of seven children.

His parents, Thomas Edward and his wife Luella, began their lives as farmers and ended their days in the small city sixty miles west of Chicago. DeKalb is also where Richard and his six siblings chose to stay and raise their Irish Catholic families as well.

It didn't take a genius to figure out that Richard was very competitive. During their daily visits, Connie would learn of Richard's athletic conquest, his card-playing shenanigans, his pool room tales, and his lively stories of escapades with brother Bob growing up on the farm.

CHAPTER 4

The Irish Connection/O'Donnell Side

We've already confirmed that my father was Irish, 100% to be exact, thanks to his parents' bloodline and their keen logical foresight to walk down the aisle with only full breeds like themselves. The bragging rights of many third-generational Irishmen continue to this day.

The spinning spiders were taking second place to only the infamous Leprechauns in the land of Saints and Scholars. The weaving of the Irish thread was headed to a new land, the land of the free, the land of opportunity.

Anthony O'Donnell and his wife Bridget Hannick O'Donnell were both born in Ireland, Anthony in 1815 in Connacht, Ireland, and Bridget in 1826 in County Mayo, Ireland. These noble and proud Irishmen were my father's great grandparents. Anthony left for America in 1849 and Bridget, his wife of four years, followed one year later. They settled in Ohio for five years until finally reaching their chosen state of Illinois, where they lived and farmed for the next forty years, bordering the county line near DeKalb and Lee County.

Thomas Edward O'Donnell Sr. (my father's grandfather) was born in Illinois along with his sister Elizabeth. Three elder siblings were born in Ireland while yet another three were born in Ohio.

Grandma Lou's Irish clan mirrors Grandpa Tom's family tree in many ways. John H. Dugan and his wife HaNorah Hickey were married on Feb. 18, 1896, in Northern Illinois. Grandma Lou was blessed with two sisters, Grace and Ruth. Grace married Clarence Buehler while Aunt Ruth chose teaching and traveling as her companions in life.

John Dugan's parents, Bernard and Mary McGuire Dugan, both emerged from the Emerald Isle in the mid-1800s. They met only once before coming to the United States. The windy city of Chicago is where they were married. They were good Catholics some would say, gracing the Midwest with eleven fine children.

My dad's parents were children of the States, both being born in the land of Lincoln. Grandpa Tom (Thomas Edward O'Donnell Jr.) and Grandma Lou (Luella Dugan) came into the new world with the fighting determination that the Irish were so famous for. They were married in 1924 and began dairy farming in the small town of Malta, Illinois. This is just a wee bit of history connecting us American-born Irish to our homeland.

From the time I can remember, there were a few things that seemed to be of importance in Richard and Connie O'Donnell's household. We were Irish, we were Catholic, and we were large, not in size but in numbers. Ten children, now that is something to make any pope smile.

Before we journey into the lives of the ten children, let's visit the molding of John Richard, the child.

The definition of "shenanigans" is as follows: a deceitful confidence trick, or mischief causing discomfort or annoyance. The origin of the word is unknown but possibly originates from the Irish "sionnachuighim," meaning "I play the fox."

T.E. and Louella's children were taking advantage of the busy farm. While the milky-haired Lou was preparing the meals and tall, lean Grandpa Tom was working the farm, the kids were up to no good. I do believe there were several foxes in the tool shed dreaming up the new and improved trick of the day used to torment their siblings and bring joy and laughter to their souls.

The girls were in the middle of the birth order, with Charlene the eldest, Joan next, and Marylou the last girl born. Charlene was the tallest, and also Grandpa Tom's pet. This may be why the sisters in question were always mischievous toward their elder playmate.

The most famous of tricks would entail the ever-abundant creature to grace most farms, the rodent. I promise, this story was shared with me personally by my "sweet Aunt Joan" with poor Aunt Charlene's confirmation, sealing the truth of the unbelievable account.

Did you know that 10- and 7-year-old girls could be so adept at catching mice? Well, Joan and Marylou made it look easy. They would borrow Grandma's gardening gloves and head off for the corn bins nearest the barn, forcing the frightened creatures right into their lair.

They would take turns; one would block the mice from escaping while the other would scoop them up just like Little Bunny Fu-Fu. Next came the delicate part, tying string to Mickey and Minnie's tiny little legs.

Off to the house they would go with sometimes up to a baker's dozen swarming around inside an old potato sack, right past dear Mom (who knew exactly what her middle girls were up to). Grandma was no doubt the keen lookout in case Grandpa or Charlene were to smell a rat, so to speak.

The four-poster bed upstairs was the short-lived home for the chosen few, at least until sundown. I am not sure what the most difficult part of the escapade was, attaching the mice to all four corners of the bed or keeping a straight face while Aunt Charlene crawled into her mousetrap for the night.

How they did it, I'll never know. Why they did it is even harder to comprehend. Aunt Joan said you could hear poor Charlene screaming bloody murder throughout the entire county. It was bad enough the younger sisters would pull such a bizarre prank on their elder, but it was so hysterical for them, they did it over and over. Aunt Charlene was well within her rights when she told me, "I hated my sisters. I could not stand them my whole childhood."

After my disbelief and utter shock upon hearing this story, my first question was, "Didn't you get in trouble from Grandpa?"

Remember, Grandma Lou was an accomplice herself, so Grandpa was Charlene's only savior. He would come up the stairs as soon as the piercing screams started, all the while slapping his belt each step he took to put the fear of God in his young hellions. By the time he reached their room, he was too busy releasing rodents one through thirteen to deal with daughters two and three. Comforting his pet, daughter number one, was all he had on his mind. I failed to ask what the brothers were doing while this was taking place. I have a feeling Dad, Bob, and Ed were rolling in their beds with waves of laughter, hoping that their creative sisters would never play this trick on them!

CHAPTER 5

The Molding of John Richard O'Donnell

Was Dad learning the tricks of the bookie trade when he was a mere child? My knowledge of Dad's childhood did not come from long talks on the front porch swing, listening to him reminisce about his childhood. That scenario would've meant Dad actually spoke to me for a long period of time. That didn't happen. The only long periods I ever had started around 13 years of age and began with puberty and a maxi pad.

A little knowledge can be a dangerous thing. This could be the real reason Dad was so quiet when it came to speaking with any of us. Luckily his sisters and brothers were willing to share.

Robert was the eldest with my father in second place out of the seven children, four boys and three girls, Charlene, Joan, Mary Lou, Edward, and baby Cletus, in that order. Richard wins the award for the best-looking O'Donnell brother, hands down. If my dad was anything, it was movie-star handsome. Yes, I am bragging about my very own father's "black Irish" good looks. This is why: it's all I ever heard! Over and over throughout our childhood, we heard from anyone and everyone—males, females, priest, aunts, clerks, brothers, and complete strangers—just how handsome my father was. Beauty is in the eye of the beholder and I guess my father had hundreds of beholders at the top of his fan club. Did his black, wavy hair, his green eyes, full lips, and lean body help mold the young Richard into the gambler, bookie, flim-flam man we all came to know? Probably so.

The adolescent Richard was too busy and exhausted working on the farm to pay too much attention to his own good looks. The dairy cows he was milking at 4 am didn't give a hoot about the great and handsome udder puller. They just wanted some release, and they got it two times per day. Nine-year-old Bob and 7-year-old Richard were tired little pups by the time they fell into bed on Rich Road. The sisters did not take over the milking until the boys left for the service in 1954. By that time, Grandpa Tom had purchased a milking machine, but the girls still had to go back and do the "stripping."

The hard-knock life of dairy farming was only the beginning, especially for the first-born sons. Dad and Uncle Bob were also expected to hunt, feed the chickens and pigs, tend to the fields, and go to school. There was no escaping the harsh and monotonous schedule or the wicked weather conditions that were common in Northern Illinois. Telling Grandpa Tom that you were tired while you pulled the quilt over your eyes in the dusty dawn did not fly. There were nine mouths to feed and clothe. The children were part of the plan, the Farmer plan.

The Great Depression was not part of the Farmer plan, but nonetheless, it happened. Dad was born in 1927. He was unlucky enough to be raised smack in the middle of America's worst economic nightmare. Fate was knocking on the old screen door. Richard, it seemed, was handed his roadmap for life. It was a small roadmap. It came in a little square package. It has a content of fifty-two, with some jokers looking on. Yes, it was a deck of innocent playing cards. The boy was hooked!

You are probably wondering what on Earth the Great Depression has to do with a deck of cards. Here is the answer: no money for entertaining means the children have to entertain themselves with games—games like Monopoly and Scrabble that came out in the '30s. I guess my dad wanted his game of choice to be at arm's length and fit in his pocket. Little Richard's first pack of cards was a gift from Grandpa Dugan, and with the gift came many lessons. Race horse rummy may have been the first game Dad mastered, but it was not the last.

Tiny gifts can sometimes make for a huge impact. This would be one of those times. I wonder if Great Grandpa had a clue just how big an impact it would make!

My father was smart. He could count cards at an early age. It wasn't that he just liked to win; winning was everything. It was never about the game; it was only about the outcome. The end justified the means in Richard's mind. He thrived on competition.

We've always heard that Dad carried around a deck of cards in his pocket from the time he started school until... well, for all we know he may have been buried with a Bicycle deck or a deck of Bee's in his suit pocket. Maybe he was hoping to play a game of poker to get his way into heaven. If there was a man on Earth that could have pulled that off, it was my dad. And I have a feeling that Dad would have agreed with that assumption and been proud of it!

The love of card-playing brought a bit of fame to Dad in high school. It almost cost him his perfect school attendance as well. It's hard to be at school when you've been kicked out.

Apparently in small farming communities like Malta, DeKalb, Rochelle, etc., card-playing was a school sport back in the early '40s. The participants would set up card tables in the school gyms, sometimes on the stage, and commence with an all-day poker match. The O'Donnell brothers were the reigning champs, the boys to beat.

They were setting up their poker table at DeKalb High School when the school principal came over and whispered to Dad and Bob, "I know you O'Donnell brothers are cheating. You've been cheating for years and I am going to sit right here until this tournament is over. I will figure out how you are cheating and the two of you will not only be thrown out of this gymnasium, but I will see to it that you are kicked out of Malta High and possibly the county, maybe even the state of Illinois!"

The game was on. "Let's see if you can catch us, Mr. Principal." It never even occurred to the brothers to just sit this one out, to let someone else win this time. Dad and Bob's reputations were at stake and by golly they were going to win this tournament if they had to get thrown out of the state trying. True to his word, the principal pulled his chair up as close to Dad and Bob as possible, his breath and eyes upon them for eight long, grueling hours.

Of course, Bob and Dad won the tournament and Mr. Principal could never figure out their method of deceit. When Layne (pronounced La-Nay) and I heard this story from Uncle Bob, we were dumbfounded. We asked Bob if they were cheating and he said, "Sure we were cheating. We always cheated. We wanted to win. We spent hours perfecting our signals. We were the bright ones. It's nothing to be ashamed of. We won and that's the point of playing a game, especially cards."

We were blinking at this point, trying to figure out what was wrong with our dad. Was this story even true? Until this story was repeated to us, we thought our father was an honest man.

Dad's older brother continued the storytelling. We believed he was getting a kick out of the looks of shock on our faces. One thing Layne and I were happy about was that Dad was not around to see our disappointment. He was too busy playing poker with God, we hoped.

The next story was even more unbelievable than the first. This time the boys had an accomplice other than a deck of cards—it was good old dad, Grandpa Tom. Dad and Bob were excellent athletes, mainly because they were fast, very fast. Dad was catching while Robert was throwing the curve balls right across the plate. No problem, except just like the card-playing episode, it was a tournament! Once again, the Machiavellian way of thinking was front and center. (Just now, it occurred to me that the three of them probably had some cold hard cash down on the game.)

Anyway, the game was tooling along. All was fine until the seventh-inning stretch. The score was getting a little tight; the boys were getting a bit nervous. What to do, what to do. I know! We will get Dad to help us; can Dad pitch for Bob? No. Can he catch for Richard? No. So what could he possibly do to help his boys? I've got it; he can be the home plate ump. Yeah, that will help! Well that was easy enough; he had already been umping the whole game. Of course, no one knew he was Mr. O'Donnell, father of the Irish twins. What harm was there really? He just helped a little. He only called one or two plays our way. We're winning anyway. Carried off the field, proud and elated was Uncle Bob, with Dad in hot pursuit.

Grandpa Tom was long gone...

A few years of this crazy behavior on the ball field worked, but Aunt Charlene remembers their Irish luck finally ran out their last days on the mound.

Someone spotted Grandpa Tom. He knew he was the father of the dynamic duo and after yet another championship win, all three scoundrels were chased off the field, running and jumping over fences into the cornfields of green. Good thing those boys could run!

Layne and I were speechless. Mouths agape. We were now getting a fairly good idea of how and why we inherited a bookie for a father, but it would be another ten years until any of us was keen enough to put it all together.

CHAPTER 6

The Courtship

If Dad would have made a wager that he wouldn't be married before he was 30, he would have lost his shirt. Mom on the other hand would have been the winner. Their romance lasted a little over a year. They were married on April 24, 1954, at Dad's home parish of St. Mary's. Mom's wish was to hook Dad sooner, but she had to become a Catholic. It was mandatory if one was to enter into the O'Donnell family.

Before they were married, Mom had done her research. She learned all the little things that might work if she was going to get Dad down the aisle. The idea that clenched it was masterful!

On Saturday nights at the Tap, Dad would be rushing around, filling coolers, and scrubbing the floors in a mad rush to get to his weekly poker game. The games were held at different places all over town; usually the locations were a much-guarded secret.

Being out of Dad's sight never settled with Mom, even if he was just playing cards in a smoke-filled room with a bunch of ruffians and whiskey all night long.

While Dad was deciding whether to hold them, walk away or run, Mom was getting herself all decked out. She was going to church with Dad at 6:30 a.m., bright and early on Sunday morning. The only problem was, Dad didn't know it! Connie had been hinting, pleading, and begging Richard to take her to church with him for months. The answer was always a resounding, "No."

Dad didn't need a reason, and Mom never got one. It was very simple; Dad was not walking into his home church in front of his whole family and most of his friends with an 18-year-old girl on his arm. He wasn't ready, but Mom was.

Imagine the shock on Dad's face when he got in his car after an all-night poker bash and found Mom sleeping in his back seat. She was hard to miss in her red quintessential suit with shoes and a purse to match. She may have been startled awake but she was ready for a fight. This time she was getting her way. She was walking the walk and it was happening soon. Dad threatened to leave her in the car. He had no problem walking the few blocks to Fourth Street. Mom said she would just chase after him in loud pursuit. That would have been a sight! Richard O'Donnell being chased down the streets of DeKalb by the young beauty in red for all the town to see.

Well, Dad couldn't be late for church—that was against the rules. Forget about what God thought; his parents would be there. It was non-consequential that he was 26 years old. He was stuck, and Connie knew it! Connie's fedora and her smile were both applied at the same moment. Around the corner and up the concrete steps they walked, never looking back.

To say some heads were turning on that sad Sunday morning was a monumental understatement. All the females who had been hoping and praying for a call from the suave and handsome town boy were now gasping and fanning themselves in utter shock. "Who was that girl walking down the aisle with Richard? Where did she come from? Why is she wearing red? What nerve." It was amazing the paramedics were not called in by Father McDonald to control the pandemonium. I'm thinking Mom was lucky she was not jumped, but then again, it *was* a house of worship.

Here is the thing; if you strolled down the aisle with a female who was not a relative back in the day, it was a done deal. She was in like Flynn. She was soon to be his wife. I've always wondered what Grandma and Grandpa thought on that surreal day. They were probably the only church members that day that sighed in relief. Dad was 26 years old. It was about time he took the plunge.

They were stunning, to say the least. Dad was decked out in a white tuxedo with dark trousers and a white bow tie. When pondering what gown Mom would wear, it was obvious she was thinking royal! Queen Elizabeth was married in 1947. It seems Connie had been dreaming of becoming the Queen of Northern Illinois! (Mom, Aunt Edna, and Aunt Gladys have always had a striking resemblance to the Queen.) Elizabeth's dress was handmade by over 350 dressmakers, among them were the embroiderers at Norman Hartnell's Mayfair fashion house. Neiman Marcus and Grandma and Grandpa George were happy to ensure that Connie glided down the aisle in "royal" fashion in April of 1954. There may not have been Chintz and Dubonnet at the O'Donnell wedding, but Mom still felt like a queen. She and Dad flew down the side steps of St. Mary's onto their royal carriage—a farm tractor—to take them on their first open ride through the streets of DeKalb, and into the most important ride of both their lives: marriage.

CHAPTER 7

Johnny

Mom and Dad did not waste any time starting a family. John Richard O'Donnell Jr. was born the same year they repeated their vows. He was a preemie, just like most of us. He lived one day. Dad left for the service fifteen days later. This was not a fairy tale start for any marriage, not by a long shot.

My own son Jordan was born three weeks early. He shared the same lung disorder as my oldest brother. The difference of course is that my Jordan lived and my husband David was not whisked away by the government, leaving me alone on the farm with my in-laws while grieving the loss of my first-born son.

Aunt Charlene and Uncle Cletus were still living at home. Charlene remembers Mom feeling very uncomfortable and very sad. She wanted off the farm, especially after Theresa was born.

Dad was given leave sometime in February, probably around his birthday. Theresa was born on Nov. 25, 1955. The wave of children had begun. Connie was a nervous wreck trying to keep up with her new daughter. Theresa cried night and day. Mom was beside herself trying to keep her crying baby from disrupting Grandma and Grandpa and the rest of the household. Mom wanted to live in town so she could hang out with the crowd over at the Tap. She missed her sisters, and most importantly she missed Dad.

The honorable discharge came a year later in October. Baby Theresa was nearly 1 year old. Mom was ecstatic to see Dad; his little girl was not. We have heard the story a million times about how Theresa did not want to share Mom with Dad. She was used to her mother all to herself. this "sharing" thing was crimping her style and she was not going to just lie back without a fight. She might have only been a year old, but she was a bright little thing. From that day forward, she was screaming out to any and all that she was the female in charge at the O'Donnell household for now and forever, amen.

Mom got her way. She and Dad rented an apartment in DeKalb on Pine Street and began the lifestyle of a newly married couple with a child. Dad was still bartending for Danny as well as filling in over at Andy's Tap when needed.

It was nice over at Andy's. Dad was the resident bookie there. There was no competition over on Lincoln Highway, so he was free to roam about the room! The basement at Andy's may have looked like a small casino. Crap tables, roulette wheels, and the ever-present poker tables were front and center. It was a heavenly place for the underworld. The Falcons Club was a mirror image to Andy's. The biggest difference was that the Falcons' basement was much larger.

Dad was a busy, busy man. Once that definitive name was attached to Dad—"The bookie"—nothing else mattered. The "book" took a slippery slide down, paying no attention to the eleven bystanders on the sideline.

If you suffer a long time without something, that something becomes the one thing you long for. It will consume you in unhealthy and bizarre ways. It becomes your obsession.

Deep within his unique persona lies a conflicted man with secrets, sadness, and self-destructive manners of unspeakable madness. Was this a sociopath/ psychopath/ narcissist we had for a father, or just a man with many addictions? I'm convinced Dad was a combination of all of the above.

If one prefers a life of narcissism, the cautionary tale of the people around you will eventually succumb to despair...

Dad and one of his brothers had snuck out to St. Mary's cemetery and buried our eldest and first-born brother Johnny in an unmarked plot. This is the bizarre account shared with me just weeks before my book was headed to publication. Michele believed I knew the story and wondered why it wasn't in my memoirs. That sick feeling was rearing up again, the feeling when your brain and body are not in sync. Even for Dad, this story was unbelievable. Two brothers in their late 20's had become gravediggers in the night. It seems Dad purchased an "old school" metal mailbox, the kind with the side flag. This was Johnny's casket, crude but inventive. The plot was supposedly in the O'Donnell family. Once again, I would channel Sherlock. I was determined to prove this macabre depiction false.

With the help of a good friend "funeral director" and the St. Mary's secretary, this unbelievable account was starting to prove me wrong. As insane as it seems, I believe this rendition of my brother's burial is true. We have four siblings buried at

St. Mary's cemetery, three are listed in the infant section in the back, unmarked. The secretary was having a difficult time finding any information concerning Johnny. This made me nervous, very nervous. She did find a note stating that Richard O'Donnell had permission from Thomas E. O'Donnell (his father) to use the site he owned to bury his firstborn son. The plot was purchased by my grandfather, but it was reserved for other family members who also gave their blessings to use the plot for our brother. There was no mention of any funeral home or date of an actual service or burial. This was highly unusual, even back in 1954. The secretary was becoming alarmed herself. Did hospitals just give deceased babies to their parents in the 1950s? We were both thinking not. When I mentioned that our cousin was the director and owner of the funeral home, the picture became clear. The note sent to St. Mary's was sent via our cousin. He was well aware of the shared plot, and more than likely, he was the temporary caregiver for Mom and Dad's precious child, at least for a while.

Again with the how's and why's. Our poor father; can this be true? I'm trying to imagine the horror, the sadness he went through, the hopelessness, the heartbreak, all because he couldn't afford a proper service and interment. Was this his reasoning? I guess we will never know for certain. I believe my mother had no idea what her young husband had done and endured. The death of her son had forced the realities of life into oblivion. Her lengthy stay at another St. Mary's facility was welcome. She was spared from the nightmare.

CHAPTER 8

The Falcons Club

The old man was always sitting on the chair, waiting. The Falcons club was his home, at least in the glass foyer for many hours per day. He was a bit creepy, but no one was getting in the club without recognition and a well-placed finger on the buzzer. We were escorted through the smoky haze immediately. Legendary bookies were always welcome, even with their kids. Mom was busy after church getting things lined up so the six of us could head down the street on time.

We usually showed up around 3:00 p.m.; that's when the music started. The first time I witnessed my mother playing the piano was smack in the middle of the huge ballroom. The curtains were open for once. It was her chance to perform. She took her seat at the piano with ease, as if she did this daily. We were in absolute shock. "Who was that up there playing that boogie-woogie music? Where were the Andrew sisters? They could be singing backup."

From that day forward, we begged Mom to play every time the ballroom was open. Sometimes they brought the baby grand out into the bar area for a special "Connie performance." She was in her element, sitting up on stage pounding fast and furious. If Dad had been paying attention, he might have been worried about being one-upped by his gal. The duet was taking place, one at the keys and one at the tables. Mom was upstairs while Dad kept busy down. The Falcons basement was a replica of Vegas with our Rat Pack father front and center!

Of course, we had no idea about the speakeasy dungeon. It was off limits to women and children. The foyer man was starting to make sense right about now. He had an extremely important position at the club it seemed. I'm certain the G-man buzzer was bigger and louder than the entrance chime we heard each Sunday. I wonder where these buzzers came from, what electrician was helping the underworld. I guess it takes a village to raise an illegal hideout. It was about time Dad got some help.

When Mom tired of playing, we were ready for a back room of our own. Off we would file with our flavored sodas in hand. The empty cigar room on Sunday evenings was our special movie room. The pizza place next door kept us fed and the orange and purple glass bottles of pop made sure we were not dehydrated during our marathon. We loved putting the quarters in the red machine that dispensed our favorite beverages. At home, all we had was warm milk and Kool-Aid. My flavor was always orange. Theresa, Michele, and Sheila chose a new color weekly, keeping it more exciting.

Lassie was our first show to hit the small black-and-white for our viewing. Oh how we wanted a dog just like her. Timmy's parents were so nice and thoughtful. We wanted that. I was forever wishing the four of us could hold hands and jump into the television on those Sunday nights, heading to the farm for peace and love with our new fluffy collie by our side.

Undoubtedly, our favorite was *Family Classics* with Frazier Thomas. It was so exciting to wait while he chose the book off his shelf. Which classic were we going to see tonight? *Journey to the Bottom of the Earth? My Friend Flicka? Ali Baba and the Forty Thieves? Born Free?* They were all equally wonderful! If you want to know how to get four O'Donnell sisters quiet, just turn on Frazier Sunday evening, close the door, and belly up to the bar and tables. You are free to roam the building for two more uninterrupted hours.

It was only an O'Donnell reunion. We never had any friends in our viewing room, just the four of us. I guess if they wanted their bookie they had to take their kids. Mom and Dad could have gone alone, and for this I thank them. It was a joy to get out, have some fun, and watch our shows without the constant loud activities that came with so many siblings over on Sixth.

You are probably wondering, if Dad did not tell any of us about his secret illegal activities, then how is it that I'm writing this account of his undercover escapades... Here we go!

Sitting with new friends in the great state of Texas one summer evening, we began discussing each other's backgrounds. Hours later when the beer and wine were about to run out, it occurred to me that my life as I knew it was a sham. Over and over in our conversation, I came to realize that my father was a member of the underworld, a member of organized crime, a numbers runner, a real-life bookie.

Gary and Carol are younger than me, but being from New Jersey, it was easy to see they were savvy, smart, and worldly when it came to the operations of a gambler running a book.

"Hey, Denise, where did you grow up?"

"I grew up in a small town 60 miles west of Chicago."

"What did your dad do for a living?"

"He owned a tavern. We lived above it."

"How many siblings do you have? What is your maiden name?"

"O'Donnell. Yes, we are Irish."

By now I can see the looks going to and from the New Jersey kids. The looks were unmistakable. They knew something I didn't. Maybe they knew something I did not want to know. But it was too late; the bookie was out of the bag, and that bookie was my very own father.

The questions continued: Did I ever see large amounts of cash anywhere in our home, did I ever see my dad on the phone writing down numbers, did my dad go to the race track, did my dad watch sports a lot, did my dad play cards, was he a member of any clubs, did my dad ever get in trouble with the law, was he arrested, did he ever know anyone who was murdered. All of these questions were answered with a resounding and tortured yes, yes, yes.

My mantra for the night was "Don't make me answer that" to every question thrown my way! Oh my God, what is happening? I don't feel good. I need to go home. I am going to get sick. Please somebody help me. This cannot be happening. In a flash, my world turned upside down. Nothing made sense and yet everything about my childhood was becoming a crystal clear reality—a reality into organized crime and into the persona I called Dad.

I had lived fifty-four years believing the lie that John Richard O'Donnell was just a hardworking barkeep. And why not? He worked hard shielding the ten of us from the underworld that dictated and consumed his life.

CHAPTER 9

Good Mom

O ur mother was our very own Martha Stewart. She was forever running around with a paintbrush or contact paper redoing and recreating a new look for our home. Thank goodness for the Sears catalog. It was her Internet, her savior. Mom also loved to entertain. She was quite the hostess with her large platters of food spread out for friends and family. Many nights she was the grand hostess, feeding and waiting on Dad and his poker buddies all evening long.

A special treat for the oldest four daughters was a candlelight gourmet dinner with just Mom. She would feed the others while we waited patiently after watching *Petticoat Junction* on Wednesday nights. Sometimes we took turns, Theresa and I at one time, and then Michele and Sheila the following week. These special dinners were exciting and greatly appreciated. Soon after Mary passed, the dinners stopped abruptly. We understood and cherish these memories in our hearts.

Mom lived in fear that someone might stop by and find her lovely home in disarray. That just wouldn't do, so instead she cleaned constantly. We had this space-age shiny thing called a buffer. It was flying across our floors day and night with one Connie Jean as the operator. The house was a sparkling testament to what Mom could accomplish, even with all those kids!

Babies were being born every year. That's what happened at our house. We never questioned their arrival, and yet my mom never looked pregnant.

Sheila wins the contest as the largest child, weighing in at a whopping 5 pounds, 5 ounces. I imagine the Salems were the main reason for the low birth weights year after year. The cigarette-smoking was something Mom started at a very early age. Dad didn't start until he met Mom. It was a terrible habit to begin so late in life. Dad learned to regret his decision, but it took a lifetime and cancer to convince him to stop.

One great benefit of the ever-present baby parade was our chance to get out of the house once a year to visit our cousins. I usually was shipped off to Aunt Joan's farm. It was my favorite place to go. We were all crazy about my dad's sisters. They were awesome. They were different. They were nice; we liked nice.

One thing I noticed right away was that they were a team, a unit. Everyone had chores. They all played musical instruments, did their homework, and helped on the farm. Uncle Bill and Aunt Joan talked to their children, kissed them goodnight, said I love you, and cleaned them. I wanted to move in and be part of the group, but no. After three days, I was returned home, along with my siblings, back to the reality of being a non-being where one was nearly invisible, unless of course, you were Theresa.

CHAPTER 10

Grandpa Tom and Parties

Sundays we would see many relatives on the concrete steps of St. Mary's, the usual suspects. The visits were short and most often it was the adults who did the speaking. I don't recall hugs or kisses from Grandma Lou or Grandpa, and no holding, hugging, or forms of expression at all between our grandparents and Richard's brood.

We grew up only blocks away and we only saw them a few times per year. Grandpa Tom would stop by to stir things up once in a while. I could hear my mother's sighs when she first laid eyes on him coming up the walk. In the door, he would appear catching our prized cat Betsy Lee within seconds. Out would come his trusty pocket knife, threatening to cut her tail off. Imagine the screams of fear and ruckus coming from the kitchen as eight children hollered and lunged at him trying to save our favorite feline. No wonder Mom made funny expressions and voices when he showed up.

When he wasn't up to animal shenanigans, he decided on gardening tomfoolery. One bright summer day, he walked in with a pocket full of half dollars. As he found a seat, Mom gathered most of us around for a quick gardening lesson from our dear grandfather.

"Now, each one of you gets one of these coins. Take it outside in a very sunny place and bury it pretty deep, keeping in mind where yours has been planted. You must water it every day with no breaks. Before long, you will see tiny little sprouts coming up. Your own half dollars will grow and you'll be rich!"

One by one, we flew out the back porch into the yard, scoping out the best sunny spot for our magnificent tree. Day after day, we would run out with our small watering cans for the daily bath. Weeks went by as we prayed for just a little hint of green in the ground. On rainy days, we would stare out the back window, hoping for our miracle tree to emerge. When winter arrived, we all gave up. Mom was never more excited for December in her life. We finally stopped asking her what was wrong with our trees and our crazy grandfather.

✠ ✠ ✠

The mole on my face did not bring me fortune, fame, or the title of supermodel. That spot was reserved for the one and only Cindy Crawford, our hometown girl that put DeKalb on the map. What my well-placed birthmark did for me was much less exciting, but it did get me out of bed and invited to my parents' parties to perform for the gang. I had two nicknames during my childhood. One was Niecy with the second being Miss America, the one that released me from my slumber to join in on the fun.

Make no mistake, I had absolutely zero clue what a "Miss America" was or why I was deemed to be one. It made no matter to me in the least. I was only the 8-year-old daughter performing my walk with a scarf made sash and plastic flowers parading through the house smiling. Oh, and the ever-famous pageant wave was a must.

Theresa was my cohort baton twirler who usually opened the show. Michele and Sheila may have taken part at some point, but I can't recall their talents at the moment.

I do recall sneaking in the free-standing wardrobe after my performance one evening. Nestled as snug as a bug on top of the winter coats. I fell fast asleep while desperately trying to stay awake. Listening to the grown-ups talk was my main mission for all the parties. The next morning brought a bit of chaos when I was missing from my bed, but eventually the double doors were opened and out I emerged.

Mom was always very excited the day of the party. She was famous for her hors d'oeuvre trays and table settings. I was especially grateful to see the pickled herring platter. I must have been low on salt and vitamin D3. They would all laugh about my loving the little fish squares, eventually hiding them out of my sight.

My mother's friend Gayle would tell me decades later how awesome Mother's parties were, saying that none of the gang could compare with the tablescapes, food, and of course, the cocktails. If the party goers arrived early, they would get a glimpse of the munchkins emerging from their baths, headed to bed. I guess that was before the sheer "numbers game" had taken over and diluted Mom and Dad's reality. Raising ten would prove to be a difficult game after all.

CHAPTER 11

The Raid

FBI did not stand for "free bets inside." At the Friendly Tap, it meant the party was over. In 1956, two years after Richard and Connie were married, the Feds paid a quick visit to Danny Kovich. The end result was a shutdown.

In the early 1950s, Estes Kefauver, a US Senator from Tennessee, was behind an investigation to crack down on organized crime. He held a televised public hearing that represented the first time the government acknowledged the existence of the American Mafia. It took a while for the authorities to find DeKalb and Danny, but not to worry, there were other taverns and more bookies on the other side of town, namely one Dick O'Donnell and the 1009, soon to become Dad's new home.

I am not sure if Danny had a back room with phones, rice paper, and big barrels of water or an operation in the basement. (Rice paper is easy to throw in water; it disintegrates immediately with all the names and numbers of the lovely clientele.) It is obvious that my dad was there during the raid and that he may have been arrested as well, but we found out that Dad had no arrest record at all, not one blemish against his name. Isn't that interesting?

The shutdown was the main reason Dad headed to the Falcons Club. With their glass foyer, keypad, and attendant, Dad was busy for a while. But he was getting tired of working and running his "book" out of other establishments. No more Andy's or the Falcons. An attorney cousin gave Dad a pep talk and the courage to rent the bar on Market. Next came the sought-after liquor license, which normally takes years with many months of prayer. Again, the luck of the Irish as well as some well-placed friends may have given the Irish farmer a full hand, with all bets in place. Dick's 1009 was now a reality, and the reason our father was MIA for years.

CHAPTER 12

The 1009/Bookie Life

Longshot, parlay, press, vig, the line, the spread—what do these strange words mean? I bet my dad knows! Yes, these are all gambling terms that consumed my dad's life. With the consumption also comes the neglect. It's difficult to be a good husband and father when your bookie gig blankets all other thoughts, feelings, and otherwise normal behavior. It takes over, one little wager at a time, until you can't remember breathing without thoughts of the "book" in your head.

In the 1940s, a new point spread came on the market, changing the way gambling would be done for decades. The spread had now been set to reflect both sides of the line. Next came the "Green Sheet" publication out of Minneapolis, which became the odds-making standard for all sports-betting in the nation. Clients paid $25 per week to receive the line service. Dad was a long-term subscriber. He needed even money on both sides of the line to guarantee he would walk away the winner. Leo Hirschfield, the publisher, made certain his weekly sheet was legal.

Together with the invention of the television and Dad's new business, the betting was easy breezy and the boys at the bar could bet, drink, and watch their sports until Huntley and Brinkley said goodnight. The trifecta had been won by all!

Dad worked long hours. We rarely saw him. Sundays we would all file into church as one large happy family. Sometimes we even got to sit next to Dad. Oddly, I do not remember if we drove the few blocks to St. Mary's or if we walked. Nevertheless, there we would all sit in one long pew. Kneel, stand, pray, up, down, listen, now speak. It's time for the sign of the cross. Now my mother is putting a crumpled-up Kleenex on my head, and here comes the dreaded bobby pin to make certain it won't fall off. Why couldn't she remember the doilies like all the other Catholic mothers? She knew it was mandated by the Catholic Church's Code of Canon law for all women, regardless of age, to wear veils or other head coverings while in the chapel. Our fashion-forward mother had set the new trend, and she was never without her tissues.

CHAPTER 13

Denise Starts School

No, not Theresa, Denise. It's Denise. "I can't get her to leave the house and she is going to be late for her first day of school." Dad didn't know what to do. He was at work and, as usual, he didn't want to be bothered with these trivial problems. Before, the pink bat phone was only used for the problem child in the household, but today it was being summoned for daughter number two.

I was getting really hot and I was tired of telling Mom and Aunt Edna the same thing over and over again. "I'm not going to school." The fear had set in. I was paralyzed beyond belief. It made no matter to me if I went to school. I was not walking myself anywhere! I was shocked at my behavior, but what were they thinking? I'm only 4 years old and you expect me to leave out this front door and find my way to kindergarten alone? Alone! Hey people, I'm the preemie, remember? In reality, I am really only 3 1/2. Not ready for school or for a walk on the wild side. These adults are just plain mad!

Even with my tiny baby brain of a 4-year-old, I could figure out this scenario was something out of a horror show. What sort of parent sends a 4-year-old to school without an adult? Why couldn't Aunt Edna take me or why couldn't she stay home while Mom walked me to Ellwood School? By the time I was to start my education, we had a house full, five children to be exact. Theresa, Denise, Michele, Sheila, and the new and only boy, 4-month-old Larry. Again, I was 4 and these things didn't outweigh my debilitating fear of being on the streets alone.

At this point, I was not crying. Mom had hung up on Dad and the two George sisters had come up with a plan. Thank goodness. I was getting really tired of standing, staring, and shaking my head. I'm not sure which sister had the grand idea of calling a family friend who had a car at the time, but that's what came next. Eddie Marshall was in our kitchen. I was whisked away in a flurry to meet and greet my new teacher, Mrs. Miller. I'm not certain how many years Eddie arrived on Sixth Street to escort the O'Donnell children over to Ellwood, but I do know it made all who made the trip very happy. Eddie would brag about taking us for years to come. The next day, I found myself walking with a group of neighbor kids, thank goodness. I don't think Eddie was up for the daily adventure.

The minute I walked into the huge brick building where I was to start my learning career, I was happy beyond belief. Mrs. Miller was the reason. She was like an angel to me. I had never seen anyone with "yellow" hair. It was beautiful, just like her. I was escorted to the yellow table with the other five students and began my daily task of arts and crafts... I was in heaven with my angel teacher!

Yellow is my favorite color and I'm wondering if this first year at Ellwood is the reason. Probably so. It's also where I learned the love of art and the love of a compliment.

I was finger painting on an easel when Mrs. Miller graced me with my very first compliment. "Denise, you are a really good painter. I really like the colors you've chosen, very pretty." I can remember being stunned. What was that? She said something that's making me feel good, feel happy. I like this feeling. I wonder if she ever had any idea how much she meant to me or how I would have preferred to stay in her classroom forever. I would be headed to St. Mary's next year, a difference of night and day. I would know what the difference between carefree and fear meant in the classroom and the schoolyard soon enough.

CHAPTER 14

Playing

Playtime was never an issue for us during our child-hood. Mom made certain we had enough toys to keep us out of her way. Our prized possessions were our Barbie dolls. We had the whole family, Ken and Midge, as well as the Barbie house, car, and accessories. Aunt Gladys would send us handmade Barbie gowns a few times each year. That package was better than any Christmas gift we ever received. Our Barbies had their own personal designer, one-of-a-kind dresses for an entire season. We had our own personal *Project Runway* starring the Missouri dress-maker, Gladys Dudley. We may have been young, but we knew those gowns were special, especially the sequin mer-maid ensembles.

In a much larger box than our Barbie clothes came our new play kitchen made of tin. We had been asking for it forever. Mom saved for one year. It was well worth it. It kept us busy for hours on end, upstairs where we belonged. Downstairs we were sequestered behind the ever-pres-ent accordion wood gates crossing the thresholds of each room. It was refreshing when we could finally step over the gates. The opening and closing to keep the younger kids out was getting old.

I suppose we were like many families. The good times and bad times wove in and out of our lives. However, our weaving had some different elements: the ever-present cloud of gambling along with a really big thread called alcoholism. Yes, I failed to mention both our parents were alcoholics. The combination of these two ailments (abuse and alcoholism) most definitely did not conjure up the makings of a loving and peaceful existence, and once the added bookie element joined forces with the dynamic duo, we were all doomed to lose the game—the game of life that is.

Finding out and coming to terms with Dad's under-world activities really opened our eyes, for most of us that is. Sadly, some are still a bit sleepy and struggling with reality. It's to be expected. It's a hard pill to swallow and the taste is horrendous. Who wants to believe their father is part of something wrong, illegal, and incorrigible? That he lived a life of lies and secrets that affected all of us, with no thought to what his decisions were doing to his wife and ten children? In the recesses of my mind, I am a bit happy that Dad did not bring us up to speed on his lifestyle choices. At least we were not forced to learn his undercover activities. I guess "I'll Raise You Ten" was only muttered at the tables. The ten of us were saved from learning the trade.

The spankings were too often and too harsh for the Fab Four and unfortunately brother Larry, but many things were questionable concerning Connie and Richard's behavior. We just knew things were not right. I guess it's time to talk about the neglect. It doesn't take a genius to figure out that one woman cannot care for ten children all by herself. Well, it can be done, but not very well. I imagine Mrs. Duggar would argue that she is doing a grand job with her nineteen and counting, but then she has help from above, doesn't she?

Mom had little faith and not much of a village. She didn't even have help from Dad. I never remember seeing my father hold or feed any of us. He was usually watching TV or sleeping when he was in the building. He was our phantom father. As long as I can recall, we were told over and over how much my dad worked. "He is working. We cannot do that. We cannot go there. We cannot do, do, do, or go, go, go. Dad is working."

So there we were, all of us pretty much stuck at the house without a driver, at the mercy of the ever-present taxi cab. Mom was in an accident when she was younger. It scared her for life from getting behind the wheel. It was just another form of embarrassment throughout our childhood we were forced to endure. Not even Aunt Edna had the sense to get her driver's license. What was wrong with these George women? Afraid to drive. It was crazy. This phobia about tooling around town was cramping the kids' style and it was a huge form of embarrassment when we were carted to birthday parties and doctors' appointments in the dreaded yellow car!

Mom was forcing me to put on a flowered sleeveless shift. I was trying to cooperate, but the pneumonia was causing me a bit of trouble. Of course, we didn't have the diagnosis until later that day. I was so sick, sweating with a fever and struggling just to breathe and stand up. I didn't think I would survive the cab ride over to the clinic. Imagine putting your 8-year-old daughter in a cab alone with a strange man who is in charge of your extremely sick child. I was very scared, but I didn't have the energy to fight. A nice woman finally asked the receptionist to help me. She could see I was about to faint in the waiting room. I was just one of many O'Donnell children that were escorted all over town by the aide of the DeKalb Taxi Company. It became the norm, but never easy.

Mom could be very fun. She loved music and she loved to dance. Her favorite was none other than Mr. Memphis himself, the one and only Elvis Presley. We would spend hours in the formal living room on our oval braided rug learning Mom's smooth dance steps.

Dad was not so blessed. He was tone-deaf and had two left feet. It was not often we saw the two of them dance, for good reason. Sheila got Mom's rhythm; the rest of us did not. I guess that's only fair since Sheila is the only one of us that remotely resembles Mom. Some say Mom had ten children because she was tired of us all looking like Dad. I don't think she minded.

✝ ✝ ✝

Our summers were fairly tame I suppose. We mainly played in our backyard. Mother May I, red light, and all forms of jump rope were our specials. Darkness brought the fireflies out, and into our jars. Why we tormented those beauties was beyond me. In the freezer, we would store the little black creatures in pickle containers. I never understood the madness behind the killing... I shudder when I remember I was part of the massacres.

Nearer to the start of school, we would walk downtown with Mom to get our new uniforms, shirts, shoes, and socks. It came in handy to be so close for shopping.

Malone's was uniform headquarters. My father's very own Aunt Grace was our personal sales lady, looking somewhat like Grandma Lou with her stern Irish chin and wavy white locks. She was upstairs ready and eager to help. If she was on commission I'm sure she was happy to see us. That's a lot of uniforms for one employee to acquire. Lucky for Mom and Dad, some years we only needed the basics. The uniforms could be let out for the growing sisters. Larry would get new slacks and shirts yearly, no hand-me-downs for the lone wolf.

After shopping, Mom would take us to a small establishment a few doors down from Malone's. The Irish bar owner treated us like royalty when we entered. Mr. Hennighan might have had a crush on Mom, or possibly he was a frequent player with Dad. Regardless, we liked the attention. The food was excellent. Time spent with Mom alone was priceless.

CHAPTER 15

First Day of First Grade

My new navy uniform from Malone's was ready with my nice white starched shirt. My ponytail was up and with Theresa by my side I walked around the corner and straight down two blocks to our new home away from home. I would have preferred Mom over Theresa to walk me into the building, but I knew better than that! Eddie Marshall had a reprieve. Michele would head to Mrs. Miller's class next year.

Coming face to face with the old maid from the card game was a bit shocking. I thought all the teachers at this Christian school were nuns. It seems I was mistaken. She stood tall and oh so straight, dressed in all gray that matched the shadows on her face and hair. My immediate comparison between Mrs. Newmann and Mrs. Miller equaled that of Satan vs. the Almighty. I hadn't learned not to judge a book by its cover yet, and I was praying my new teacher would prove me wrong.

The first thing I was asked to do was find my name tag on the bulletin board. I guess arts and crafts was all

I learned over at Ellwood after all. I was frozen once again in fear, knowing that I was probably the only 5-year-old that didn't recognize her own name. Mom and Dad believed the learning was to happen only in the school building. No Head Start for me as I began my Catholic education. If I would have had a crystal ball on that first day, I would have rushed out the door and into the nearest cornfield I could find and hid behind the stalks until high school.

The first oddity that occurred during my incarceration in Mrs. Newmann's first-grade class was my nose bleeds. Who knew that the combination of debilitating fear combined with nose bleeds would equal the beginnings of a wicked first year and beyond? I sat in the middle of the third row, out of sight of the teacher. The others alerted the old maid that it had happened again. "Denise has another bloody nose. Mrs. Newmann, she's bleeding again."

The bleeding started at the beginning of my first year and lasted until the end. I can still see myself sitting in my school desk, awakened by the outcries of my classmates as the blood ran down my face and my jumper. Not again, oh no, not again! Just like that, *bam*. I was back in the hearing world, and not very happy with the sounds.

Sometimes I would wake up in the classroom, but then there were times I would find myself on Fisk Street headed home. My crimson face, uniform, and hands were my first clue that I needed a wash and a change of clothes. I was always shocked each time I came out of my blank state. It was very frightening; although by mid-year I was getting used to the episodes. These episodes I kept to myself. I was hoping someone would notice the signs of trauma and abuse... They did not.

I did wonder how I managed through the busy intersection right outside my classroom. Luckily, it was a school crossing to keep me safe. It's difficult for the deaf, dumb, and blind to navigate if even for a short while.

In the screen door I would walk. Mom would usually be in the kitchen. She was never happy to see me home for my afternoon quick change. At least she didn't shake me time and time again like Mrs. Newmann. I would be hauled down to the lower level basement by my arm. Sometimes I wouldn't wake up until most of the shaking and yelling had subsided. "Denise, you have to quit this. You know what I am talking about. Now go home and change and get back here right away. This had better stop, do you hear me?"

Crying never happened during these horrific events. I just flew home like a boomerang. What was she talking about anyway? I wasn't causing my nosebleeds. I was not picking my nose. I really wasn't.

Several months spent with Mrs. Newmann brought a much worse tragedy for not only myself, but for the entire world. The blood was running. It was not my lifeblood that was flowing; it was the blood rushing from a gaping wound in the President of the United States' head. It was a Friday afternoon in Mrs. Newmann's class. A day most Americans will never forget.

Suddenly there was a rush of activity, bells ringing and all students being filed into the church next door. We had no idea what was happening. We were thinking maybe this was a tornado drill or the Russians had landed. Of course, we were keeping these ideas to ourselves. The more obvious sounds were that of teardrops and soft sobbing. The Sisters were bawling uncontrollably with balled-up tissues to stifle their sounds as we were escorted into the pews to await the announcement.

We all learned quickly on this November afternoon what the meaning of death was about. Our head priest announced that the president of our country had died.

Prayers were said in unison, with many extra Hail Marys, before we were all told to go home. As we walked down the grand steps of St. Mary's, many teary-eyed parents had already arrived to escort the masses of children home.

When Theresa and I spotted each other, we headed down our well-known path to find our mother in the same situation we had just left. Mom was on the sofa. She was rocking and bawling in front of the television. We had never seen a teacher or nun cry, and now we were staring in disbelief that our very own mother was doing the same thing.

I can't imagine any other chain of events that would lead us to witness an entire school getting released early, with priests, nuns, teachers, and parents rushing around like crying zombies. Killing our thirty-fifth president, John F. Kennedy, our youngest president in the land, would do it. For heaven's sake, he was not only our youngest president, he was the first Irish Catholic president. He was our hero, especially to those of us who shared his thread of land and religion.

I turned 6 the day after President Kennedy's assassination in 1963 when our Irish Nobleman (king of Camelot) left us. I was certain nothing could cause my mother to react so violently again. In a few short years, I would witness the same rocking and crying, enhanced and followed by shrills of unstoppable guttural screams that made the infamous day in November seem calm.

✟ ✟ ✟

The blood clots that formed in my throat from pinching my nose while my head was tilted back were becoming more heinous for all to endure. They were especially disgusting for me since I was the one spitting them out daily. Finally, Mom decided she must get to the bottom of my nosebleeds. Mrs. Newmann had made the pink bat phone ring, so the next phone to ring was the doctor's office over at the DeKalb Clinic. The big, tan, brick building was waiting as Mom and I walked up the curvy sidewalk the Saturday following my birthday.

What a glorious gift. A cauterization of my nose tissues had taken place in record time. The bleeding had been mitigated almost immediately. It was such a simple procedure that relinquished a mountain of trauma from my young life. Praise Jesus, my prayers had been answered.

The blanking out and the stares from my classmates had stopped, if only for a short while. Don't get me wrong, I was beyond ecstatic when the bleeding stopped; I just wasn't ready for the next oddity that was to meet me at the end of my first year.

Richard

Connie

Mom and Dad's wedding day   *Family of eight*

Mom in mirror on wedding day

Baby Denise

Mom, Dad & Theresa. Mom was pregnant with Denise.

Denise & Stevie right before I left for New Mexico

Dad & Mom, one of her last photos with Dad

First home on Pine   Our home on Sixth Street

The 1009 Tavern   A rare find of Dad on the
                         opposite side of the bar

St. Mary's School.
Bottom left windows—
where I spent 2 years.

St. Mary's Church

Denise on steps of 1009
Tavern, 2018. Building
now apartments.

St. Mary's Hospital
where Denise was born

Mom and Edna's look-a-like-The Queen

Easter Sunday, Mom & Dad

Aunt Edna

*Left to Right:
Edna, Connie, Gladys, Doris*

*Mom, Dad, and
the nine children*

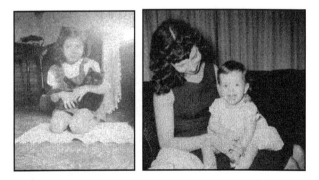

Mom & Kitty   Mom & Denise

Dec. 1960 Christmas. Back
Row, left to right: Denise,
Theresa. Front Row, left
to right: Sheila, Michele.

Denise & Theresa, Easter

Denise & Theresa   Denise's third birthday, 1960

Michele Sheila Larry; Lisa

Layne Tina Yvette Steven

Aunt Edna Uncle Red & Aunt Gladys

Theresa, St. Mary's, second grade

Denise, St. Mary's, first grade

Denise, fourth grade

Dad at Sheila's wedding

Dad, Mom, Michele & Russ

CHAPTER 16

The First Year Has Ended

The April showers had brought in the May flowers as I skipped home on my last day of school. The air was perfect, with just a light breeze that carried the aroma of lilies as I was turning the corner on Fisk. I was so happy I was free of the old maid, her flat ugly face, and her mean demeanor. The woman loathed me. I could feel her hate seeping into me all year long, like dirty soap water into a sponge. I didn't care what nun was to come next, any penguin would do.

Humming the new tune by Lesley Gore, ''It's My Party,'' I rounded the corner. Mom, Sheila, and Larry were all waiting for us. Theresa beat me in the house, but only because our next-door neighbor, Edna the flower lady, stopped me in my tracks. "Let me see that report card, missy." I was not supposed to open it or allow anyone other than Mom to see it, but I was not accustomed to telling adults no. The old gardener took the white envelope from me and glared at the contents. Her head lifted, slowly, very slowly, and the look of bewilderment was my reflection back at her. "Well, I'll be darned. You had better wipe that grin off your little face. You are not advancing into second grade."

What? What does "advancing" mean? What was she saying? I could tell whatever she was saying was not good. I took my report card back and home through the screen door towards my mother. "What is she saying? What does this mean?"

The dreaded words came out of my mother's mouth as her cigarette was dangling: "You are not going into second grade, Denise. You are being held back in first grade for another year." No, no, no. The tears were instant. This could not be my fate. I just could not fathom spending another year in that horrible woman's class. I don't remember falling to the floor in a hysterical heap, but I do remember my dear Aunt Edna picking me up.

I was staying back, and they knew. Once again, I was acting a bit like my older sibling. I was making a fuss. "Oh, please Aunt Edna, don't let them send me back to first grade! I can't go. I can't go."

"Connie, why didn't you tell Denise earlier she was being held back?"

Mom was standing now, folding laundry at the kitchen table as usual. She made a funny face at her sister and shook her head, as if ordering her silence. It was too late; I heard what she said! "What? You knew I wasn't going into second grade and you chose not to tell me?" My mind was telling me this wasn't right; what was wrong with the grown-ups in this house? I was adamant. "Why didn't you tell me and what did I do wrong to warrant this punishment?"

Mom was forced to actually look at me and speak. She told me I wasn't learning as quickly as the others and 1 more year would help get me up to speed. I was thinking, speed is the only attribute I have. I was always picked first on the playground for red rover and dodge ball. This was not the speed she was referring to. My new classmates would soon explain exactly what this "catching up" was all about.

The repeat of first grade was not going to ruin my summer. The upcoming year would be bad enough. Let's have some fun while it lasted. Outside was the place to be. Theresa, Michele, Sheila, Larry, Lisa, and new addition Layne were the motley crew running around Sixth Street the summer of 1964. We had a nice backyard with a large swing set and, of course, the plastic swimming pool was a must. Susie and Mark and the Clarks from across the street were usually around.

We toured the street, having a blast at each home we landed. The nicest home was two doors down on the corner. It was a huge white home with a massive wrap-around circular porch. It was a multi-living residence like many from that era. Grandparents and children living side by side. They had standard poodles that were amazing animals. Grandma P. would call us over for cookies regularly. She didn't have to holler twice. Her cookies and her canines were equally wonderful. Her out-of-state grandsons would arrive mid-summer each year, becoming instant members of our group.

I liked staying outside. There wasn't any cigarette smoke hovering over me. Mom was basically a chain smoker. I guess she wanted to have that in common with Dad and Aunt Edna. The Kilauea-like cloud of smoke was ever present and became worse when Edna and Dad returned home each night.

When forced to go inside, I preferred dancing with Mom in the formal living room. She would open the large accordion gate that separated the dining room from the "off-limits" living area a few times per week. "The Devil in Disguise" was the Elvis song of the summer. Elvis's devil was a woman; mine was not. I learned soon enough it was much better to sing about the Devil in Disguise than look him directly in the eyes!

My peaceful summer was coming to an end. A crystal ball would have been helpful, or a parent that watches their children. I would have taken either.

CHAPTER 17

The Big Boy

The fireflies were waiting. How I wish they could have lighted the skies above, tiny little stars showing me my path home. The world was so very dark when he let me go. Many fears surrounded me at this moment. My tears were still falling and my chest was still pounding. Disoriented, I was trying to remember how I got this far from home and why I was allowed to stay out alone in the night.

It was a game of hide-n-seek. "Let's hide from everyone. Let's get under the porch." I didn't really want to crawl under the creepy steps, but he was nearly an adult, so like always, I conceded.

Immediately, I realized I had made the wrong decision. "What's happening? Why is this big boy on top of me? Why is he tugging at my clothes?" Instinctively, I knew I could not go to my "blank" place; I needed to fight! The screams and kicking took over; the lashing of my head back and forth was explosive. It was the only thing I could think of to keep his sweaty face and lips from hitting me, again and again. I may have only been 7 years old, but I knew this was different from any abuse that had come before. I was in a state of full, overwhelming panic. He was trying to kill me. I was fighting for my life. And then, just like the onslaught, it stopped.

The darkness was waiting for us when we crawled out from under the stoop. In a few steps, he was inside his door and I was alone. I'm sure I was a sight. Disheveled clothes, muddy, tear-stained face to match my tainted soul. My face and clothes could be cleaned. The spirit of my little being was the bigger issue. How long does one have to wait for that cleansing to occur?

I was free. I needed to start moving, moving towards home before he came back. Looking down, I could see my feet shuffling. Keep going, Denise. Just one step at a time and soon you'll be safe. A few obstacles stopped me in my tracks. Between the ebony night and my 7-year-old sense of direction, I was lost, very lost.

I walked around and around, down one street then another. I did not recognize any of the houses. There were zero landmarks to guide me to safety. How did I get so far from Sixth Street and my family? I had just saved myself, from what was not exactly clear. The dim moon was not my friend that evening. The darkness was enveloping my vision and my spirit.

I have no idea how many minutes or hours I walked in circles. I was exhausted and scared beyond belief. What if another boy is waiting in the shadows to pounce on me? Why are these thoughts seeping into my brain? I had to find my way home. And then, there it was. A house I recognized. In a second, my relief turned into horror. Oh my God, I was back at the monster's lair.

The guttural moan came from a place deep within. My lips were quivering and the panic was back in full force.

To this day, I cannot explain to you or to myself how I took the steps one at a time to his front door and knocked.

I stared at the pavement. My fear was much too great to look him in the eyes. His constant muttering and begging me not to tell anyone kept me in the present. The "I am sorry" over and over again kept me a prisoner. It occurred to me that he knew where I lived. How odd. His apologies sounded sincere, and he was nice enough to take me home. My quiet voice would keep him safe for a while. His hiding was secure.

Once I began to see familiar surroundings, my breathing was resurrected. Maybe I would live after all. With my dear Cape Cod in plain sight, he turned and ran. The little girl was home, and the big boy was gone.

The fanfare screams of excitement welcoming me through the door were nonexistent. "It's about time you came home. We were starting to worry about you." Seriously, that's what she said. Unbelievable. No questions about my late-night escapades, no questioning about my well-being. Were they blind? Could they not see my dirty face and how distraught I was? I guess the answer was a resounding no.

I was sent to bed without food or a much-needed bath. It was never spoken of again. I figured they just didn't care and I didn't know how to put in words what had happened.

The silence takes its toll. It will catch up with you. I would soon learn that silence is not always golden, but I had a plan. My plan would take a while. I would bide my time, perfecting my redemption. The old maid and the big boy would not destroy my remaining days of summer.

The playing and swimming continued, and we even had a special trip to a drive-in movie. How many kids can you get in the back of a station wagon for outdoor movie watching? I'd say at least five with an infant in someone's arms. That was a really good night. Family gatherings didn't happen often. I don't remember the title or the stars. It didn't matter. We were ecstatic to be in our footy pajamas lounging in the backseat pointed at the large screen. We knew when these rarities occurred, they should never be forgotten.

On the way home, we stopped at Dog-n-Suds for black cows. This adventure could not have been any more perfect. We could have used more days like these, but life always seemed to get in our way.

CHAPTER 18

Sixth Street/Theresa

If any of the neighbors were to peer through the windows while we were living on Sixth Street, they would have probably thought, "Yes, the problem in this household is with the eldest child, Theresa."

That's exactly what the rest of us thought as well. She was out of control. That was easy to see, but did anyone wonder why?

"Emotionally disturbed" was Theresa's diagnosis when she was finally seen by a DeKalb psychiatrist around the age of 7. He referred her to a mental health center in Chicago, a live-in facility. He told my parents her mental health depended on professional help immediately.

Connie and Richard never considered it. No walking, no running, just hiding and pretending. Now that was a clever move, all right. Aunt Edna said that Mom was afraid people would think Theresa was retarded, so the decision was made to do nothing to help the child.

What about the rest of us? Did we not deserve some peace and quiet in our lives? Once again, did anyone see the bigger picture here? Anyone! The answer is yes. Aunt Edna was an artist. She could see the finished painting and it was not a Picasso. She did not wield enough power to turn the painting into a masterpiece. Not even the best brushes and paints in the world could help her now. We were, without a doubt, on our own; we were our own worst enemies. Enemies that stay quiet, regardless of what was happening in their war.

Knives were Theresa's weapons of choice. I remember escaping from one of her tirades around the age of 5. I was chased around our oval kitchen table, with Mom in hot pursuit of Theresa, Theresa in hot pursuit of me, and screams abounding on all sides. I leaped on top of our roll-away dishwasher that sat in the corner and performed some quick-learned Irish dancing until Mom could get the knife away from Theresa. I don't remember what I did to deserve such attention. It was just another part of my day, a day with the oldest.

Was this one of the times Dad would come home late from work or the racetrack and wake Theresa up for one of her "spankings"? Mom would of course threaten all of us with that very real possibility. Who does that? Wake up a sleeping child to give them a spanking? And make no mistake, at our house to call it a spanking was questionable. To this day, I get uneasy when I hear change in someone's pocket jingling around. It was our first clue to tighten up and get ready for the big leather belt to be slipped through the loops and find its way to our tiny little bodies, blow after blow. If only there would have been somewhere to hide. We needed somewhere to hide.

What sort of mother did we have? What was wrong with her? She never once stepped in and stopped Dad from hitting us. Never! I remember begging her to not tell Daddy. "Please, Mommy, don't tell him. We will be good." It was as if she could hardly wait until he got home to watch her children suffer. How she could just stand there and listen, I'll never know. I will never understand what was going on in her mind while her husband was altering the lives and souls of their children, and possibly the lives of their future grandchildren. The madness usually finds a way to continue, like cockroaches. It lives on and on and on.

By default, I was struck many times just by the mere fact that I was lying next to Theresa. I should have allowed Michele or Sheila to sleep in the full-size bed with her while I climbed into one of the bunks. I've since learned that I would rather be hit myself than listen to someone else's screams. I still have nightmares about listening to my siblings' cries while I can do nothing to help. Being helpless in one's dreams is almost worse than being helpless while awake. Almost.

The helpless were everywhere.

To protect the innocence and privacy of others, I will keep these next identities a secret. I was staying overnight with some people while I was fairly young. I was around 10 years old. We were all tucked in bed when some commotion and laughter was heard from the bedroom on the end, the bedroom with the girls. The giggles continued from the lively pair, and the next thing that was heard was not laughter; it was a warning that one of the girls would get sick. At first I was confused. How could laughing with your sister cause one to get sick? Over and over, I could hear one person and then another repeat the warning, "You better stop. You know you will get sick."

It wasn't long until I understood the meaning of "sick." Up from the bedroom came the dad, headed for the room with the dreaded belt in one hand and a wastebasket in the other. Slap, screams, throwing up, slap, screams, throwing up. On and on it went. Noooo, this is a new horror even for me. Please stop hurting my friend! Stop making her throw up. Please stop. Why is everyone just lying in bed listening to her father beat her? My nightmare was following me, only I was awake and not at my own house.

It wasn't even my father hurting my sister, it was my best friend's house. But wait a minute; if this was real, if this was actually happening at their house to their daughter, then I guess this happens in all houses to all daughters. Yep, that's it. This is normal. Oh, thank goodness—I was beginning to think I had monsters for parents.

Did I go home and mention any part of my waking nightmare to my mom and dad? Of course not. I may have been young, but dumb I wasn't. Why on Earth would I think they would care about someone else's child when they were on the same team as her assailant? Yes, this was the 1950s. I understand there was a different mentality back then when it came to disciplining one's children; however, I wonder how many parents pushed the limits of what was humane during this time. I guess the monsters were free to continue the art of terror and fear to whomever and as often as they liked, especially if they were Mom and Dad.

Were we in fear daily at my house? Yes. Did we get spankings every day? No. But it was enough to crush the innocent spirits of all who slept at 423 North Sixth Street in the quiet farm town of DeKalb, Illinois.

I am certain by now you are wondering, what on Earth was wrong with Richard and Connie? Or you may be convincing yourselves this could not possibly be true. Let me assure you of two things: It is true and I don't have the complete answers to why our parents, the parents we loved so desperately, were the way they were.

There were many unwritten rules coming from the constant stream of abusers. No guessing what was to be kept quiet and what would be shouted aloud for the "others" to hear. The monsters were smart enough to scream the rules from the tops of their lungs. Sometimes there was even Show-n-Tell. There were mind-numbing visual effects to make certain the special ones kept quiet, mouths kept clenched for eternity, or so they hoped.

The alcohol was my mother's muzzle and companion through life. It began around age 14 and lasted until her early death at age 50.

Dear Aunt Edna was our main source of information concerning her younger sister. She was more than happy to share Mom's secrets with us girls. She told us Mom started drinking around the age of 14. Edna says Mom would hide vodka in small jars at school. This was shocking to us, but we didn't learn about the sexual abuse until decades later.

Now, her afternoon beverages were making sense. With limited knowledge about our father, we had to stop and wonder. We have heard that Grandpa Tom would take the boys to the barn with a large razor strap whenever they were out of line. If Dad was the bearer of any other forms of abuse, it was a secret he took to his grave. His reasons for drinking were probably multifunctional, with the number one reason being the bookie element.

CHAPTER 19

Second Year of First Grade

Out the door and around the corner once again. The walk was slow. I knew what was ahead. The air was still a bit heavy. The crisp fall breezes with radiant colors had not begun. Luckily, I hadn't grown too much. I could wear the same jumper as the season before. The diamond patch on the top left corner blazed the three initials I dreaded the most, SMS—"St. Mary's School." My little beanie was without adornment. At least at school I was safe from the Kleenex headdress. There was no need for Theresa to walk me into my building. We parted at the entrance.

She looked even more menacing than the year before. Possibly she'd had a traumatic summer like me! Once all the new children had arrived and located their names on the bulletin board, we waited. I skated through the embarrassment of finding my name, since this year I recognized it right away.

The red face and shame were only seconds away. I should have known! I was sparring with the she-devil, St. Mary's finest!

"The first place we will go, students, is on a small tour of the building. The lavatories will be our first stop. Denise and Roger were here last year and since they know the way to the restrooms, I will have them show you the way. Roger and Denise, come up to the front and wait until everyone is lined up behind you before we begin."

From that moment on, we knew what "catching up" was about. Within days, my cohort and I were both labeled "the stupid ones."

"Denise is dumb. Denise is dense. Roger is a retard." Kids could be so cruel, but then again, they came by it honestly. They were taking notes from the best.

I survived my second year of first grade. Things were coming to an end. I watched in horror as many others were chosen for the abuses the adults were so eager to hand out. I witnessed my classmates being hit, pushed, shoved, thrown down stairs, and ordered to dark, damp cloakrooms as daily punishments. Was it right or fair to see bloodshed at school administered by the "sacred" faculty? I was beginning to understand that fair had little to do with children. At least not on this corner, at this school, in the 1950s and 1960s.

I kept my head down and watched as Mrs. Newmann chose the new wave of students to berate for her entertainment. My nosebleeds had stopped and I was catching up. She was on to greener pastures. My bathroom buddy Roger sat helplessly while the entire student body was ordered to walk across his feet. Thirty-three in single file, all stepping and stomping as ordered. His punishment for tripping Mary Ellen Fitzgerald by mistake. He was also sent to Sister Mary Jerome's office for whatever expert terror she could inflict. I did my best to block most of the abuses out of my mind.

I was the happiest on art day or when reading in the "star" club group. I loved to read. My favorite subject was social studies. For a long time, I wished I could be an Eskimo. I was entranced by their lands and their ways. I dreamed of moving to Alaska. I could see myself in my fur-lined parka in a tiny little boat searching for my Moby... Finding peace and harmony with my tribe would bring me home. I was ready.

Instead, I was walking home with Theresa, headed for another vacation. My past summer would not be repeated. I was very careful these days and my plan was getting honed to perfection. I wonder if the big boy knew he had picked the wrong O'Donnell girl to attack. God and time were on my side.

In the parking lot of the DeKalb hospital, several sisters and I were approached by none other than Mrs. Newmann one cloudy, rainy afternoon. Her sister was a few doors down from our beloved Aunt Edna. The cancer was taking Aunt Edna very quickly. We did notice it was our former teacher passing us in the hallway, but no words were spoken until she came upon us outside. She addressed us as "O'Donnell sisters" as she began speaking. We were all transfixed into stone, just staring, waiting for what on Earth she wanted with us. In a few short minutes we were dazed, confused, and bewildered. Mrs. Newmann stood in the parking lot after forty-plus years and apologized to us O'Donnells, just like that. She never actually muttered the word "apologize," but the message was clear; she felt bad for the way she had treated us. She said she was a new teacher and had no idea how to deal with "some students." Then she told us something really shocking: "I never, never attend any of my students' parents' funerals; I made this decision at the beginning of my career. I've only released myself once from my hard, fast decision and that was to attend your father's funeral. The moment I saw your dad's obituary in the *Chronicle*, a strong voice in my head said, 'You are going to Richard O'Donnell's funeral.' I just thought you girls might like to know this." It was a unison out-of-body experience for the four of us. I cannot remember much after this except getting into our car and driving away, as our first-grade teacher was standing in the parking lot alone, staring at us in the rain.

CHAPTER 20

Tommy's Bike Shop

Another rite of passage in the summer was our surprise outings with our mystery father. Out of the blue, Dad would order one of us to get in the car. It was only one child at a time and we never knew until we parked on Lincoln Highway that it was our lucky day.

The next thing you knew, Dad was saying, "Pick out any one you want, any color, any style." My choice was a classic blue. Theresa had already gotten the cool purple model the previous summer. I always wondered how we could afford brand-new bikes for all of us kids. Come to think of it, Tommy never looked too happy to see Dad walk in the door. I guess Tommy knew exactly how we were paying the bill. Luckily for the ten of us, Tommy liked to play the horses. His horses never came in, but out the door our bicycles would go each summer with happy little O'Donnells in tow. It was a good day, a new form of transportation and a few precious moments with Dad.

Theresa and I would race around the block all summer long. We would leave our front sidewalk, pointed in opposite directions, and race wildly back to our starting point. The fun part was when we met in the middle. This gave us a clue as to who was going to win. More often than not, I was the champion racer, which never sat well with big sister.

I was learning quickly that winning felt good. It was of no consequence to me that I would pay for all my competitiveness later with hair-pulling, kicking, and screaming from Theresa. Most of the time, she tired of chasing me. Good thing I inherited Dad's speed. It sure came in handy when it came to survival with the crazy one.

Jordan and Valerie would beg for "Aunt Theresa" stories when they were young. Forget *The Monster at the End of This Book*. My sister was the monster they wanted to hear about. By the time my kids were 5 and 4 years old, I was running low on her shenanigans. I was nearly ready to make some up, but then the memories started flooding in.

One of their favorites was the bang-cutting incident. How many times we all had to witness this over the years, I do not recall. It was madness. For whatever reason, Theresa hated to have her bangs trimmed. The last trimming was as chaotic as the first. Why did my parents never learn?

There was a kitchen chair, a belt, scissors, a mom, an aunt, and a child. It was a cold December day with mounds of fresh snow on the ground, piercing screams inside, and sisters rushing after the eldest daughter. Either Theresa was chasing someone or being chased by an adult in charge; it was just the way. Today she had been caught. The belt barely made it around her and the wooden chair. She wasn't getting away this time.

Aunt Edna started in with the snapping scissors just as Theresa jumped up with the chair still attached to her waist. Out the door she flew. The blizzard-like conditions didn't bother my sister. She was flying free, right down the sidewalk with a kitchen chair attached to her bottom. Around the corner, no shoes, no coat, no problem. Imagine what the neighbors were thinking! By now, they were probably waiting for the entertainment to begin.

A phone call came in for Dad. I think this time Mom used the bat signal as well. He ignored all forms of communication. The women were on their own. The freezing weather finally brought sister to the back door, pounding to be let in. The chair was gone, most likely in pieces along the path. It seemed like an hour, but I'm sure it was only a few minutes until Mom let her through the pink laundry room and into the warm, safe kitchen. The blank stares were coming from the siblings with mouths agape. We had become accustomed to her behavior!

Jordan and Valerie never tired of this story. They would laugh and laugh with unbelievable sounds of joy each and every time.

CHAPTER 21

Second Grade, First Communion

My personal old maid was finally being passed to another player. I was headed to second grade.

Pointy headdress, black and white, and holy all over was my new savior. Weighing in under 100 pounds, Sister Mary Greta was the new nun on the block, ready for the class of 1965 with one O'Donnell behind the desk.

I really liked her. She was very pretty and usually had a smile at some point throughout the day, which was not always the case with most of the emporers.

The most exciting thing happening this year had nothing to do with my teacher. It was all about the priest and my vengeance on the "big boy." I was getting a beautiful mini wedding dress with a matching veil, shoes, rosary, Bible, and the opportunity to become the bride of Christ. The holy Eucharist would seal my new beginning. I would soon emerge with Jesus for eternity.

There were months of preparation. My mission was nearing completion. My main concern was not all the regalia preceding the ceremony. Don't get me wrong, I was ecstatic with the attention my walk down the aisle would obtain, but all this was just secondary. The focus of this young girl was revenge. I was determined. My plan was in sight.

It may have been Theresa's hand-me-down communion dress, but everything else was new. My favorite item was my little white Bible with the gold ribbon. My scratchy dress and tight shoes were unbearable. Thank goodness I would be out of them soon. The three of us drove the two blocks to St. Mary's. Mom and Dad deposited me with all the other tiny brides and grooms. The heavenly show was starting.

I have a hero in mind. I must wait for a while until I'm spiritually able to speak with him. He has a white collar and sits in a small booth with a sliding wood panel. Yes, it's my very own parish priest. He will need a little help from above and a bit of help from me. Together, the three of us will stop and punish the big boy in his tracks from hurting more innocent children. He will pay.

Out of the pews one row at a time, we headed to the kneeling bar in the front of the sanctuary. The mass was fairly typical except we were way closer to our priest than ever before. Years later, the wafers would be placed in our hands, but for now we were sticking out our little tongues for the priest, but ever so slightly.

We were special enough to be escorted to Father O'Connell before the congregation and now we were filing back into our seats. Catholicism means something now. We were worthy of the name. Blurting out our sins in the confessional would be our next big sacrament... And part of my plan.

The food in the church basement was delicious and it was fun seeing some relatives, but I was ready to get out of my attire and head home. My next adventure was waiting.

Today was the day. I was shuffling with the others headed through the playground to the chapel. "Bless me, Father, for I have sinned. These are my sins." That's how it starts. Once the priest has slid the screen across, it's now your turn to speak. Most of the others were a nervous wreck, wondering what on Earth they were going to say, making up sins so they didn't look ridiculous. I knew exactly what I was going to say. I'd been practicing for over a year.

"I kissed a boy." Those were the four little words that were going to save me from damnation and punish the big boy simultaneously. The priest would absolve me for my sin and send up a request to God to punish the boy. All was good! I had thought about it for over a year. I was so happy. I wouldn't have to tell anyone, no parents, no teachers, only the priest. He would never know who I was.

My plan was perfect. I was so proud of myself. I only knew the word for kiss, but I was certain the man of God would figure the rest out. I felt so icky after it happened. It had to be a sin, one of the really bad ones. No more thinking about it or him. I was free.

And then it happened. My freedom was short-lived, only lasting a few seconds. No, no, no. What on Earth is happening? Why is Father O'Connell out of his box? Why is he glaring at me? For heaven's sake, he's almost touching me with his robe! He's not supposed to see me. This is my secret and now he's here, right next to me, staring. Doesn't anyone wonder why he's out in the open? This is all so wrong. I want to crawl into a corner, hide my face, and die. My biggest sin now has a face to go with the horror. It couldn't be any worse unless it was the Pope or God himself standing next to me!

I was frozen, stunned. He was not speaking, only peering. I finally moved and got back with my classmates for the short walk next door. Bad things stick with you over the years. This one was imprinted in my mind with a laser. It was never going away. I absolutely hated confession from that day on. I never trusted a priest again. Never!

I was still praying that my God would punish my attacker, because that is what God does. He punishes bad people. I had asked for forgiveness, so I was off the hook, even if Father O'Connell had messed it up for me.

Looking back, I always wondered why he came out. Just why did he have to see who I was? He never did anything to help me other than take my unsanctioned confession. I still get sick to my stomach when I think of my tiny self in the confessional, whispering my terrible sin through the screen. Believing I was safe and hidden from human condemnation. Once again, I would be utterly disgusted and disappointed by yet another "grown-up." This one was a bit harder to grab ahold of. I thought the collar was above this kind of behavior. My 8-year-old mind was failing me again.

CHAPTER 22

Tina and Larry

O ur troops were headed to Vietnam while Julie
Andrews was portraying a singing nun on the big
screen in 1965. The immediate concern at our house
was new sister Tina's survival. She was another preemie, weighing in right under 4 pounds. I don't remember where I was shipped off in April for my yearly stay,
probably Aunt Joanne's again. I wonder who took care of
her kids when she visited the hospital for her babies. They
never came our way during her seven deliveries. I suppose
she figured Mom had enough on her hands.

When asked what his middle name was one Sunday,
Larry replied, "Larry Marie." I thought my dad was going
to kick him down the church steps in front of everyone.
Poor Larry. He had heard many times how we all had the
same middle name... All the girls that is. How Mom knew
she was going to have eight girls is a mystery, but she started

with Theresa and carried it through. Lawrence William soon learned his second name, and he was unlikely to ever forget.

I would have liked to have forgotten all the head-banging I witnessed from our one and only brother. He was a tantrum-throwing boy of great regularity. We would all watch in horror as he slammed his head on the floor in front of the stairs, sometimes the wall would suffice. Mom and Dad would just wait until he was finished. They never seemed concerned. As usual, I knew this was not right, but keeping my mouth shut was becoming my learned response.

✞ ✞ ✞

No treatment can reverse the impact of alcohol on your baby's health. And no treatment can make the effects less severe. Being one of the eldest born to Richard and Connie was a blessing. Living outside Mom's womb for the last three months of incubation was an added miracle. I suppose that sounds cruel. What a horrible thing to say. The truth can be a hard pill to swallow and, like I stated earlier, living the lives we were handed did not help the medicine of life go down easy. It seemed to be going at a snail's pace. The daily grind was slow, but ever-changing.

Premature babies, brain disorders, and mental and emotional issues were all clear and present dangers that had attached themselves via the umbilical cord to the ten of us. The latter children were the very unlucky! But we are a determined Irish clan that would rise up and revolt. It was in our genes to go up against the establishment. Our forefathers would expect nothing less.

Mom and Cleo would be sitting patiently for my return with the big and heavy paper sack. Dad was always pacing on the front steps of the 1009 when I appeared. Immediately, I followed the path back to Sixth Street to the waiting ladies. The red cans were icy cold, the popping tops were very welcome, the best friends were smiling now as the liquid and foam found their home. As usual, it took me a decade to put two and two together. I was bringing the mothers beer in the middle of the afternoon. Unbelievable!!

Soon I would be free from the heavy lifting. When school starts, the taxi cab driver and the next-door neighbor will be summoned as the new errand boys, but they will be going to the real liquor stores, not the Tavern. This was a well-kept secret for years. Mom was a determined woman with an addiction that needed to be fed. A move of disastrous proportions was on the horizon. It would prove to be the worst idea our parents ever had.

And now there were eight.. Children that is. Theresa, Denise, Michele, Sheila, Larry, Melisa, Layne, and Kristina. Why didn't I pay more attention to my younger siblings during our childhood? They were just kinda there. I don't remember changing their diapers, helping with their bottles, or doing anything at all to help Mom with all the little ones.

Mom was a do-it-yourself gal. She was always moving. Never in my life did I see her sit down with us for dinner, not once. She transferred most of the food into bowls, then she stood ready to grab anything we needed. The pots and pans were sparkling clean before we had poured our gravy.

Asking, "May I be excused?" was the only time we spoke while at the table. "How was your day? What did you learn at school? Have you done your homework? Do you need any help with your homework?" Nope. Only silence until we finished with our plates. My entire life I just wanted my father to say "No, you may not be excused." I paid attention, hoping for the no. I didn't care if it was my no or another's. It's a funny thing. Why was I so focused, so obsessed about this strange suppertime dance we had nightly? A few times, I purposely left mounds of food on my plate, and that didn't work either. He still said, "Yes, you may be excused."

Including this dinner talk, I probably didn't speak one-on-one with my dad for more than eight hours in my entire life. After I was married, he would call around 2 a.m. after the bar closed. These phone calls were a welcome surprise. I looked forward to hearing his voice, even if he was usually drunk when I answered.

One early-morning my husband David finally said something to Dad about the odd, early morning chats. The calls stopped immediately. I didn't blame David. He had to get up at 4 a.m. daily, especially when he was the plant manager. I believe Dad was insecure. He needed to be tipsy and have uninterrupted time for conversation. I will cherish each and every phone call, holding on to the special moments we had as father and daughter, even if they were short-lived.

CHAPTER 23

Sister Mary

How absurdly ironic that in January of 1966 Sonny and Cher were singing "I Got You Babe" while Herman Hermits were simultaneously belting out the popular tune, "Can't You Feel My Heartbeat."

Mom and Dad were at St. Mary's hospital expecting the same real-time sentiments once baby number nine appeared. Our problem was, the doctor was not.

Mom's labor pains usually went unnoticed until she was heading out the door. We would be sent the next day to the relatives' with Aunt Edna's help packing our suitcases for the four-day trip. It was very exciting to arrive home to meet our new sisters. The idea that a boy might appear was nonexistent. This year, things were very, very different. Mom returned empty-handed. No sister, no surprise brother.

I had just turned 8 in November, so I knew what death was all about. We had buried several kittens in our front yard under the hedges over the past summer. We watched as momma cat, Betsy Lee, continued to walk the house in circles and sniff the dirt out front, searching in vain for her sweet, black, furry babies. Mom did a great job explaining to us about the cruelty of Mother Nature. It never crossed our minds we would be relying on Mom's well-rehearsed education of death so soon.

The story was, the doctor got stuck by a train, a long train that had to back up time and time again. He finally arrived (in a tuxedo) as the horrified nurse met him with the devastating news of delivery. Mary was born alive, but died very quickly. The exact details were never disclosed. We had a sister to mourn and bury. The accusations were up to the adults.

From the relatives who were suddenly bringing us home early to the quiet, blank stares from our parents, we had never seen such sadness. We had no idea what was going on or why we were being deposited ahead of schedule. Aunt Edna was in tears when we walked through the door. How tragic for her. She was beside herself with grief for our sister and for her younger sister alike. Looking back, I'm so grateful for Aunt Edna. It would have been unthinkable for Mom to carry the burden of announcement herself.

The world keeps turning. If you are the mother, you have no reprieve. You must carry on. We were on our best behavior, sensing our role in the family. Being good was all we could offer. Dad had his own demons. Squelching one was on his radar. When the hospital bill showed up, Dad wrote on the bottom: "I don't think so. No train." Dad's research paid off. There was only a clear track on January 26, 1966. A train was not the obstacle. Showing up in his party tuxedo while on call was not a grand idea for any obstetrician, even if the alcohol had already worn off (the on-call doctor was not Dr. Feeney).

The O'Donnells had learned a valuable lesson: Alcohol can kill. It's only a matter of time and it takes many forms. The form with "past due" never arrived. The physician kept his license but realized the hard way: Don't gamble with Dick O'Donnell. You will lose one way or the other. We heard rumors that the delivery nurse quit her job, never to return to any hospital again. The trickle-down effect of substance abuse is forever flowing, seeping in the lives of whomever it chooses.

CHAPTER 24

Missouri Vacations

Our Missouri trip was scheduled the summer after Mary's death. Mom needed some comforting from her parents, so we loaded up the station wagon and headed down Highway 38. With Aunt Edna, there were eleven bodies in the car. Good thing we were tiny people; otherwise Aunt Edna may have ended up on the roof in a lawn chair!

The four oldest sat in the back, facing traffic. Everyone else was scattered about. No seat belts, no air conditioning, windows down, and three smokers in route to Auxvasse, Missouri, for a few fun days.

As "My Baby Does the Hanky-Panky" was blaring from our trusty transistor radio, the car radio was giving play-by-play action of Bollo and Tommy John. Maybe this year the White Sox could make Dad some money and bring his home team some notoriety. Dad didn't like the hanky-panky tune. We were ordered to turn it off. We thought the song was about a gal waving around a handkerchief. What was the big deal anyway? We didn't argue. No reason to pull the car over. No reason at all.

The Country Squire was on drive mode until we pulled in to Grandma's driveway. The great anticipation of the day was crossing the Big Muddy. We never tired of seeing that magnificent river down below. We were blessed with our very own Mississippi black water beauty and we knew it was a special moment each and every trip.

Grumpy Grandpa George scared us a bit, but Grandma made up for all his brashness. She always looked like a grandmother. White hair, dusters, slumped over, and fluffy. We never witnessed Grandma in a pair of pants, always snap dresses. Mom was a change-of-life baby. Beulah was in her mid-forties when she arrived. I guess she was tired of all the hoop-lah with dressing up daily. It was no matter to us. We adored her.

The trailer was small, so we were sent to relatives during our stay. It's not likely that many can accommodate a baker's dozen. Theresa always headed to Uncle Billy's in Jefferson City. I was lucky. Uncle Red liked me so I was sent to the farm. Aunt Gladys and Uncle Red never had children, we were not privy to the reason why. As I was sitting on the hard teal sofa bed awaiting the childless duo, I was told over and over again how fortunate I was that Red liked me, I was going to the "rich" uncle's house for rest and relaxation.

Sometimes others came along with me, but more often than not, I was alone. I adored the peace and quiet. The front porch was my favorite room. I spent many quiet hours reading my Perry Mason and Nancy Drew mysteries while swinging back and forth on the antique metal glider. The warming sun coming in through the screens helped with my daily afternoon naps. The cocoon-like effect I was surrounded in was heavenly. No chatter, no screaming, no cloud of cigarette smoke. The fresh breezes and the sounds of nature combined with my sought-after isolation were priceless. While lying in bed at night, the whippoorwills were my Streisands.

If only I had been warned of their omens of death and bad luck to all that listened. On the wings of angels, I would have flown into the safety of the midnight sky.

The summer of 1966 would prove to be a difficult one for one small 9 1/2-year-old girl named Denise.

The vultures were circling. One on the farm and one at the bar. Once again, I was the prey that attracted predators with no ability to escape. The bartender I will not dignify with a name. The landowner was married to my mother's sister, Gladys. The monster went by the nickname of Red. It matched his hair and his evil demeanor. Forgetting both their ugly faces would have been welcome. In the busy daylight, I can turn away. It's the many night terrors over the years, forcing me to relive and remember. The blanking out doesn't follow me into my slumber. I surrender unwillingly, if only until dawn, grateful for the sunrise and a new beginning.

By this time in my short life, I had learned to fear the present and the past. I was praying the future would bring only peace.

Aunt Gladys knew exactly what her disgusting mate was doing when he followed me to the basement for frozen strawberries. What crazed power was he wielding over her for her to engage in this perverted activity? It shouldn't take this long to open a freezer and return with a bag of fruit.

The volume on the upstairs television suddenly was blaring to deafening heights. My screams were obviously being drowned out. No reason his accomplice needed to hear the cries of yet another female in the house. All was good upstairs. She was busy watching her shows and adding a lazy daisy stitch to her embroidered pillowcases. What a wonderful life for the crafty and wealthy down on the farm, as long as you were an adult that is.

The twisted pair had a devious plan. They knew I wanted desperately to go fishing. I'd talked about it non-stop over my previous vacations. For days after the base-ment incident, they had tried every which way to get me alone with Red. I knew what they were doing and I wasn't putting myself in that situation again! I was not going to the barn to see the cows, I would not go to town to get treats, I would not ride to visit the neighbors. My answers were unequivocally no, no, and no.

One evening, I was told that the three of us were going fishing on the property... I was safe at last; there was no way any harm would come my way if Aunt Gladys was present.

We were all up bright and early, busying ourselves with the fishing gear when I noticed Aunt Gladys didn't look ready for an outdoor activity. She was in the mid-dle of homemade cream puffs that require hours of spe-cialized baking. The fear was starting; the sweating and heart-pounding were immediate.

As I was backing away from the kitchen, shaking my head and professing that I was not going, I became the trapped mouse. Red had taken off work to take me; how dare I be so disrespectful to think I could just change my mind? What an impudent little girl I had become. Think of all we have done for you!

Walking out the back porch, I'm surprised they couldn't hear my screaming prayers for salvation. I remember nothing of the fishing and molesting expedi-tion. I'm happy for that at least. What I do remember was the gutting of the fish and chopping of their heads upon our return. They were placed on an old tree stump while

I was ordered to watch, all the while being told how easy these knives could be applied to humans. Humans with big voices and tall tales for all to hear.

I wasn't a wounded or disfigured animal, but I certainly did attract predators. I was a magnet for the men, the monsters. I've wondered over my many seasons just what was there about me that caused this attention, unwanted and unwelcome. I suppose if one is neglected or looks too tempting or innocent, the men become the attackers, pouncing day or night whenever the evil invades their minds and my body! My guardian angel must have been sleeping throughout my childhood. Or maybe there were just too many little girls and boys to save. Was this the reason my prayers went unanswered? In the play of my life, I prayed desperately to be free from the men. One day it occurred to me to pray for the others. I hoped that I didn't personally know any of the other helpless souls being watched, stalked. More importantly, I was praying I wasn't sharing an address with any.

Connie was forced to pretend at a fairly young age; she had no choices in the matter. Mom went to live with her sister Gladys and Uncle Red when she was in junior high. They lived close to the only school in the county. How fortunate for the deviant homeowner; his prey was moving in and staying a long time. Mom never told us she was molested by Uncle Red. Remember, she was a master secret keeper of many sins. Some belonged to others, and some she owned. If only she would have talked, it might have changed the course of history for those of us who came later.

Fish guts and fish heads with my image appeared over and over again for days. Now it was time to go home. I was very, very quiet as I sat staring out the big window. The sounds of silence were dancing in my head, trying to make sense of the people I trusted. This would be the case for decades, especially when I learned of Mom's past fate while living with the Dudleys on the farm.

How could she let me stay there with him, with her? What kind of mother was she? I still get angry when asking these questions. It had become clear that wondering does no good.

"Shikata ga nai" is a Japanese phrase and cultural concept. The phrase means, "It cannot be helped" or "Nothing can be done about it." I believe my path to enlightenment began at a very early age, possibly at conception. The Four Noble Truths, which Buddha taught, are the following:

- The truth of suffering
- The truth of the cause of suffering
- The truth of the end of suffering
- The truth of the path that frees us from suffering

Collectively, these principles explain why humans hurt and how to overcome suffering. Unfortunately, these principles were not part of my vocabulary until recently. Remarkably, there is still time.

CHAPTER 25

Swimming and Speck

"Hot Town Summer in the City." We were now allowed to ride our bikes to Hopkins Park for pool fun. It was quite a trip from our house to Sycamore Road, but we were young and had no problem pedaling a few miles each way. The best part of the journey was the underground tunnel that channeled beneath the highway, right up to the pool's front door. Without this ingenious and fun structure, we most likely would have been killed while crossing traffic. My new yellow Velcro baby doll swimsuit was the best article of the summer. It was a sassy seersucker ensemble.

Noon would be my mark for peeling the front panel off for the remainder of my swimming pleasure. I was determined to have a tan belly like the others. Our book latches were used for towel racks as we flew to Dairy Queen with our trusted quarters in hand for a well-deserved cone and a bit of rest.

I had no problem keeping the terror, violence, and abuse in my young life away from the media. The remainder of the world this summer was not following in my footsteps. Six thousand American troops were now in Vietnam, China's Cultural Revolution had begun, the subway strike in New York brings the city to a halt, and Charles Whitman kills fourteen and injures thirty-one on a killing spree at the University of Texas in Austin.

Dad's nightly sports watching was being overruled by the killings. A little over an hour away, there was a barbarian of untold horrors lurking closer to home. Nearly two weeks into July, Richard Benjamin Speck would be arrested at Cook County Hospital after being recognized by a young surgical resident. The physician called the police after noticing the "Born to Raise Hell" tattoo that had been pictured in the papers. (A suicide attempt brought the slayer to the emergency room.) The murderer of eight young nursing students, who struck on July 13, 1966, had been apprehended. The City of Chicago could now take a breath. A maniacal Richard had been taken off the windy streets for good. Speck's death couldn't have arrived early enough for the families of the nurses and the residents of Illinois. He died at age 50, on his birthday. The country welcomed his heart attack and his journey to hell.

CHAPTER 26

The Bartender

I guess I was spotted by the nameless bartender while helping Aunt Edna in the kitchen. I was oblivious to the attention. Dad asked me if I wanted to ride over to Sycamore with his worker. It seemed he needed a female to help choose the perfect Mother's Day gift. These monsters are clever, very clever!

I didn't want to go. I told my father I did not want to go. Again, I followed orders, slowly walking out the tavern door and into his car. We headed down Highway 23. By now, I was conditioned to be aware and nervous around male adults, especially when alone and helpless.

The endless country roads and cornfields are abundant in our county, hiding more than spiders and field mice when necessary. This day in May, they were hiding the Evil and the Innocent. My innocence was slipping away quickly this summer with no chance of salvation. I would always wonder how many pure little girls would become part of this demented agenda. Too many to count and too many to save. I was only a child myself; escaping was not an option.

I remember the beginning. No middle or end. My blanking out was serving me well.

When I reluctantly presented my mother with her very own gemstone pin, I'm certain she had no idea the price her young daughter paid for the butterfly beauty. There were two mothers living in oblivion on that special day, never knowing the stench of evil that was attached to their shiny creatures of the sky.

CHAPTER 27

We Never Talked

Icannot remember ever talking about the spanking episodes with anyone, not even each other. We just went back to sleep or back to playing or went to church. It didn't matter. We just went on. Only once did any one of us speak the unspeakable, and that's because she was asked.

Sisters saving sisters. This is what changed the tide. Praise Jesus we were Irish Catholic. Without knowing how they intervened, our usually "mean" nuns from St. Mary's School became the O'Donnell girls' saviors. Remember though, they had a little help from Mom's sister, Aunt Edna.

Seventeen years Mom's senior, Aunt Edna was always the constant steady in our home. She was a strong woman, physically and emotionally. The Cherokee bloodline borrowed from Grandpa George showed through on Edna, which was in stark contrast to her younger sister, the Heddy look-a-like, Connie Jean.

Keep in mind the nuns were not our friends. We feared them 100% of the time. Poor Michele, I imagine she was scared to death. You don't lie to a nun. No way. Little sister Michele wasn't headed down the highway to hell. She was singing like a bird, and the birdie had a lot to tell.

Michele was singled out because she had a black eye. The belt buckle decided to land somewhere that could not be covered up by leggings. Dad was in motion once again. Theresa and I were getting spanked, desperately trying to escape, cowered in the corner of our small day bed when Michele came to our defense. She was hit by the heavy buckle during a backswing.

When the nameless nun asked, "What is that mark on your face, Michele? How did you get it?" she told the truth. The nun actually walked Michele home from school that very second. Two blocks later, Mom was staring at Sister Mary, someone in full headdress, banging on her front porch door. This servant of God was looking for answers, and just like us kids, Mom was not going to lie to a nun about Michele's black-and-blue eye. She told the nun the mark was from the belt buckle. She tried very hard to make the incident seem much more innocent than it was. Protection mode was setting in.

When Dad and Aunt Edna found out about the nun visit, things drastically changed. Aunt Edna was adamant that the beatings were going to stop. She convinced Mom and Dad that the children they created would be taken away, and more importantly the town would know what was happening over at the two-story green-and-white Cape Cod. Constance stopped the tattle-telling and John Richard kept his belt in the loops.

Facing the shame was never an option for Dick and Connie. What would Grandma and Grandpa O'Donnell think? What about Dad's sisters and brothers, the priest, the neighbors? The gang down at the Falcon DeKalb was much too small and unforgiving for this to get out. Yep, the kids were finally getting a reprieve from the madness, if only for a while.

CHAPTER 28

Bath Issues

The first thing to happen when being deposited at either Grandma Lou's or one of our beloved aunts' was a bath. (Once, Aunt Marylou bathed me in the kitchen sink.) After looking back, we can agree: No surprise there. Between the haze of cigarette smoke, body order, and dirt, we didn't stand a chance from the stares, ridicule, and laughter from teachers, nuns, and peers. Did the ever-flowing liquids Mom and Dad were drinking keep our baths at bay, away from the sea of suds, or was it the sheer numbers of our constant growing brood? It doesn't take a genius to realize that one woman with nearly zero help can't take care of ten children properly, not by a long shot.

Our filthy appearance was a constant stream of shame that followed us for years. Even now, I shudder when I think of what we must have looked like. Picture day was always welcome during the school year. The night before was always a "bath night." I'm sure the St. Mary's staff was elated!

Wonders of wonders, my next oddity was in the future. By the time I started third grade, my previous nickname was switched from Stupid to Stinky. I had begun sweating profusely under my arms. Why do these things keep happening to me? The "whys" in my life were becoming long and lucid. I just could not catch a break!

I wore my green sweater every day to keep the sweat stains from the others' stares, but it didn't help the odor. The congregation of children kept me aware. They never wanted me to forget I was the smelly one. Every day, I would hear their taunts and see the looks of disgust on their faces. I would just pull my green cape tighter, look away, and count the seconds until the bell rang.

CHAPTER 29

Skipping School and Encyclopedias

Theresa was striking out. She had been caught several times this month. I guess she wasn't as smart as all the doctors were saying. As she was slithering down the neighbors' upstairs apartment, she was spotted by Cleo and returned home.

Theresa had decided she was no longer needed at school. The Beasleys all worked, and they never locked their doors. Sounds like a place to hang out all day if you are a 12-year-old St. Mary's runaway. Watching television, snacking, and napping were all worth the belting she received when Dad got home. She loved all forms of attention. I tried to warn her, but listening to her younger sister was not her style, not then and not now.

Actually, doing the wrong thing again and again over the years has been her mantra for life. As I've told her many times, "This is the definition of crazy." The only difference being, she knows things will stay the same. She is not really expecting a different result. Theresa Marie has always craved the crazy.

The bed was small and it was freezing. The baby brigade was still marching on. With no more room, the makeshift porch was now our sleeping quarters. We could hear the television from our bed. It was right outside the door. Let's grab the encyclopedias from the bookshelf, put them in our pajama bottoms, flip over, and start making a fuss. Dad will come in with his trusty belt and spank us, but we won't feel a thing. The green-and-white books will save the day. Sounds like a great plan to pass the night away. Well, it really was priceless. It worked exactly according to plan, my plan! Yes, it was all my idea! I'll never forget the chuckles from Dad when he figured out what we had done. He was proud of our shenanigans and I was so excited, I shouted my creative accomplishment with glee. To this day, I'm not sure he believed me. I guess I do have a wee bit of the Emerald Isle coursing through my veins after all. I was channeling my aunts, Grandpa Tom, and Dad all with one swift Irish move on a cold winter's night.

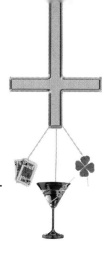

CHAPTER 30

Maria and Rusty

Two ordinary nights would end tragically for one small girl and one young man in the small towns of Sycamore and DeKalb. The 25-year-old bartender was a good friend of Dad's; the child was not. Maria Ridulph was taken on December 3, the year of my birth, 1957. Rusty was found on the floor of the Falcons Club on Friday, September 15, 1961. In five short years, these sleepy sister towns in Northern Illinois would find fame and misfortune in the most macabre ways imaginable.

An innocent game of "duck the cars" between best friends would be the last time the girls saw one another alive. As the snowflakes fell, they were approached by a 17-year-old male asking if they wanted piggy-back rides and candy. Kathy ran home to get her mittens while Marie left for her doll. When Kathy returned, her playmate and the man had disappeared.

Kathy immediately returned to Marie's home with the shocking news. At first, the parents assumed she was hiding, but after an hour the police and armed civilians began a search of the town. Two days later, the State Police as well as the FBI descended upon Sycamore and its meager residents. President Dwight D. Eisenhower and FBI Director J. Edgar Hoover took an interest in the case as well as the national media. Two tourists were searching for mushrooms near Woodbine, Illinois, about 100 miles from Sycamore, when they discovered the remains of a small child. The four months of praying and waiting had been excruciating for the parents and townspeople. Based on dental records, the body was confirmed to be that of Maria Ridulph. The chilling lack of evidence led to a fifty-year-long cold case for the prosecutors of DeKalb County.

Then, like a midsummer's dream, a deathbed confession from the killer's mother was ultimately the tip leading to the arrest of Jack McCullough in 2008. No DNA was recovered after little Marie's body was exhumed, but the jury did convict McCullough in 2012 for the kidnapping and murder of Maria Ridulph. He received a life sentence with the possibility of parole after twenty years.

McCullough continued to scream his innocence over and over during his five years of incarceration. In April of 2016, DeKalb County Judge William Brady agreed. The convicted murderer was released at the age of 76. New evidence surfaced supporting McCullough's alibi. He was now a free man.

The ruling for Maria's family was one more tragic event in the line of missteps and false hopes. When could they put their beloved and beautiful child to rest? When would this nightmare be over?

This senseless murder has made a lasting impact on most of our nation throughout the years. For those of us geographically nearer to the abduction, things become a bit clearer. Personally, for me they get more frightening. DeKalb and Sycamore are only six miles apart. One can barely tell when you've crossed the city limits. If this horrific murder could have taken place in Sycamore in 1957, then yes, it can happen anywhere. Could the killer still be free? Roaming the streets of our county? My abduction happened only seven years after Maria's senseless death. I will always be grateful I was not killed. The teenager who stole my innocence could have very well quieted me forever, just like Maria's abductor. My heart goes out to that precious child. I know the fear firsthand, the terror! Why her, why not me? What's wrong with these men? Why are we surrounded by monsters?

Fruitless questions with no true answers. If any lessons are to be learned from these two tragic incidents, let it be shouted from the rooftops, "Parents, watch your children."

CHAPTER 31

Moving Across from Gayle

What are the chances of moving in across the street from Rusty's widow decades after his death? If I was a betting being like my father, I would have said zero. As my sister Sheila says, "You can't make this shit up." That's exactly correct. Gayle was directly out my front window waving for me to come over. I had no idea who she was until she mentioned her previous name of Moore. As I turned a greater shade of pale and nearly fainted, my husband David came to my rescue.

Introducing him to Gayle was a bit dangerous. It was now his turn to change pigment while trying to stay upright. Remember, we had become aware of my Dad's involvement in the underworld a few short years ago, never dreaming we would now be living just steps away from Rusty's dear wife and son. It's no wonder she didn't ask what was wrong with us. What would we have said? "I think my dad may know a lot more about your late husband's murder." These words never reached her ears. She died never knowing my ideas and concerns about Rusty's demise.

Gayle wouldn't have believed one word of what I was thinking. She would have been angry beyond belief. As I got to know her over the few years we had left, I truly learned to cherish our friendship. I can say without hesitation, I loved and respected her immensely. She wasn't an easy friend. She was extremely opinionated, very political, and very prejudiced, not in that order. I learned a lot from her and cherished our time together, regardless of her boisterous personality. She put up with my incessant talking, story-telling, and calamities, so the friendship worked liked clockwork.

I made her countless meals that she greatly appreciated and she taught me how to stick up for myself time and time again. She was the most intelligent woman I've ever met, sharp as a tack and not afraid of anyone or anything. She made me laugh daily, and that in itself was priceless. She was my elderly best friend, sassy in her classic blue-and-white signature outfits with her daily glass of wine by her side. She is greatly missed. I look forward to meeting her again someday. Hopefully she won't be too upset about my writing by the time I'm headed her way.

Gazing out our front window as Gary our neighbor scurries back and forth tending his lawn, the thoughts of his father weigh heavy on my mind. Gary was only 3 weeks old when the murder occurred. In a few horrible seconds, a beautiful mother and son were now without a husband and father because a lone gunman was on a desperate mission. The killing of Rusty was much more personal and proved to deposit the dripping bloodshed closer to home.

The murderer was after the cold cash. He waited patiently at the bar, pretending he was interested in his last cool glass of beer before the other barflies headed out. His mission was to be alone and ready before Rusty left the Falcons Club towards the safety of the bank a few short blocks away.

It was a .25 caliber Italian-made automatic that was used to shoot Rusty around 12:30 a.m. on Friday, September 15, 1961. Rusty had only just become an employee of the Falcons Club a few weeks before his ill-fated life came to an end. If any mistakes were made on his part, it would be counting the money in front of a patron. Richard O'Donnell had taught him better than that. It was never to be done. But Rusty wanted to get home to Gayle and his new infant. The man at the bar looked harmless enough. Looks and intuition on that particular morning would prove to be the dead opposite for the newly hired bartender at the Falcons Club.

The entire town was buzzing over the senseless murder within hours of the slaying. My father was hauled to the police station immediately for questioning. I remember all the whispers and talk years later about my dad's dealings with the police after his friend and coworker's death. Mom lost track of how many times Dad was "asked" to come in for questioning. There was always a "why." Why did the police want to talk to Richard over and over again? Was it because he trained Rusty in the trade or was something else going on? Was that trade bartender, bookie, or both?

Three shots to the back of the head and another two in the face was a bit excessive for a robbery. Seems like the townspeople and the DeKalb police were thinking along those same lines. Dad was very cooperative, but didn't really add anything new to the investigation. They finally stopped hauling him downtown. Dad was smart to be quiet. It could have been him behind the bar that early morning, and he knew it!

There are two conflicting stories, one from my dad and one from Gayle the widow. Dad says he called Rusty earlier that day asking if he would take his shift. The racetrack was calling Dad's name and he needed a favor. Gayle says the bar manager Lupinski had been the one to switch nights with Rusty, not my father. I learned of this discrepancy in 2011 when we moved across the street from Gayle. Dad had died in 1999. I believe he would, without question, have stuck to his story, even if it wasn't the police doing the questioning.

Becoming a female friend of Gayle's was not easy, not in the 1960s and not in the 2000s when I came back to town. Mom and I should consider ourselves very, very lucky and extremely blessed. Many women prefer the company of men. Gayle was the headmistress of that club undoubtedly. Rusty and Gayle were a striking couple. With her chiseled Norwegian good looks and perfect size 5, she turned heads when entering a room. She was a snappy dresser. Even in her seventies she looked put together most of the time. Her blond hair was remarkable, soft like clouds, the way she demanded. Rusty had rugged good looks with reddish hair and the ruddy complexion that follows the reds so often.

Mom was a different kind of beauty, with her light complexion and deep ebony locks that she was known for. Dad had the waves most men hated, but they served him well. Together, the foursome was just happy to dress up and have some good times. They usually decided on the upscale Fisherman's Inn a few miles from DeKalb, or a quaint spot in town. Gayle tells of one particular evening when she took a liking to the ashtray on the table. She went on and on about the blue-and-white ceramic beauty, but Dad could not convince the young waitress to hand it over. Usually his gift of gab and his charisma could secure what he needed, but not this time, not with this gal. Gayle really didn't expect the tray to go home with her anyway. It was a long shot for sure.

Dad hung back while the car was being pulled around and damn if he didn't get in the car a few minutes later clutching a brown doggie bag for Gayle. No, it wasn't food. It was her new modern ashtray ready for a new home. They all were in disbelief. Even Mom was shocked by this turn of events. Dad of course played the gift and his acting debut down to a few short words. He was not one to give up his secrets or his modus operandi.

CHAPTER 32

Rusty's Killer

Ronald Popov was arrested just one day into the murder investigation of Rusty Moore. Popov was the last person seen in the company of Moore at the DeKalb Falcons Club. He denied his involvement during the early stages of his interrogation, but soon recanted, stating that he did indeed shoot, kill, and rob Rusty for the money deposit in the drawer. There was also cash in a safe, which was never touched by Popov. He admitted to hiding the $6,000 in the bottom of an elevator shaft in a storefront on East Lincoln Highway, DeKalb. The gun was taken apart by the killer following the murder and was never found. Popov then, without coaxing, reenacted the gruesome killing in detail. The shots fired fiendishly aimed at Rusty's eyes were a particularly horrid account he seemed proud of.

The lone killer was found guilty on December 29, 1961, headed to life behind bars for the next ninety-nine years. The state had done its duty. Another murderer was behind bars. Should there have been others headed to

Stateville along with him? To this day, that's a grand question that's still being asked.

What did Dad know about Rusty's murder? Dad knew the chief of police was a dear friend of Gayle and Rusty's. That was the first piece of the puzzle most of the town was aware of. When Vic Sarich shows up at your door at 5:30 a.m. to personally give you the shocking news of your deceased husband, the friendship is obvious. Dad helped trained Rusty, so he was dumbfounded when learning that the cash was taken out of the till while Popov was still in the building. Why did Dad really ask Rusty to fill in for him? Was our father the real target on that infamous early morning, or was he just following orders?

There was a rumor that Popov also applied for the same bartending position as Rusty and may have been upset when he was passed over. Do you kill someone in cold blood because they secured a part-time job you wanted? I don't think so, and neither did many others.

Why shoot the bartender? You have a gun in his face; you are the only two people in the huge building. Why not take the money and run? Instead you shoot him several times in the back of the head, then flip him over, then shoot two more bullets into his face to make certain he's dead. All this after he has made the call for his police escort to the bank. You don't bother with the money in the safe at all. Instead you rush to downtown DeKalb to hide the $6,000 cash in an elevator shaft. For hours you sat at the bar in full view of all the remaining patrons who could point their fingers in your direction. A masked hold-up could have kept your identity hidden. You could have been a free man with a wad of cash. Instead you give yourself up in less than twenty-four hours, ending up penniless with ninety-nine behind bars.

Joe Friday would be saying, "Just the facts, ma'am." The problem is, the facts are too old, too few, and too hidden. Once again, let me reiterate: My ideas are mine and mine alone. I have contemplated for years, wondering about my father's involvement. Did Dad know anything about Rusty's upcoming death? Was he threatened himself because of his own activities with unsavory individuals? Ultimately, these questions don't have an air-tight alibi. The motive will forever be suspicious conjecture on my part, and possibly on the part of my readers. Maybe I've read too many Perry Mason and Sherlock Holmes books in my lifetime, followed by a flurry of detective shows fueling my skeptical mind.

Nonetheless, a decent and good man, husband, father, and friend was wiped off this Earth all too early, with the ease of a madman and his Italian-made gun.

CHAPTER 33

Danny

Every year we waited in anticipation for two things at our household: Christmas and a new baby. The year 1966, when I was 9 years old, we had an early Christmas gift. It was a new baby brother. Yes, a boy! Mom spent her 32nd birthday in the hospital. At 32 years old, Mom had already been pregnant twelve times. So far, she hadn't needed to share her December 18 birthday with anyone. Danny arrived on the seventeenth, allowing Mom to keep her special day all to herself. We didn't mind Mom being away on her birthday. We were having a grand time staying with our cousins. This year on the eighteenth, we were all watching, *How the Grinch Stole Christmas*. The debut of Dr. Seuss's children's classic coming to CBS for the first time was an added gift for our viewing pleasure. This year was beginning to look a lot like Christmas. The only thing missing was a good snowfall to complete our magically awaited December!

Danny was another preemie, weighing in under 5 pounds, but he was healthy enough to come home way before Christmas to join our big O'Donnell brood. The atmosphere was joyous for all. Remember we were still in mourning for our sister Mary who passed nearly 1 year from the day of sweet Danny's birth.

Aunts and uncles began depositing us around December twentieth. Mom and Danny arrived shortly thereafter. Yes, we were trying to get used to this anomaly, a baby boy, but it was all good. Mom was overjoyed with a healthy child to carry home in her arms, as well as a brotherly gift for Larry.

The place was crowded. Danny made nine, and remember we have Aunt Edna living with us, sleeping in the makeshift freezing front porch/bedroom. Kids were sleeping on sofas, sometimes four to a bed. There was a continual crib in Mom and Dad's room that was a permanent fixture, for good reason. The three "real" bedrooms were cramped beyond belief, but that didn't stop the baby brigade. Dick and Connie would make it work.

Good Catholics had as many children as the good Lord would provide. It was the way.

What does twenty-one days mean? It could be the best twenty-one days of your life; it could be the worst days of your life. For us, it meant the days of our brother's survival. Nothing more, nothing less.

Funny how crystal clear tragic events sear themselves into your mind. I can recall the night of January 7 like it was yesterday.

Dad's feet hit the floor at the bottom of the stairs. He was checking on Danny. The second we all heard the thud, the screaming began, especially from our mother. I don't think you could really consider it screaming. It was more guttural, a sound I had never heard before that night or since. Dad was rushing for the phone as Mom was racing upstairs. She didn't need to hear any explanation. She was a mother tiger trying to save her cub. She was unsuccessful.

I remember the card game we were playing at the kitchen table. I remember Mom's bright pink negligee and matching robe. It had feather-like trim on the arms and bottom. It was draped around her and Danny as she lay on her bed, wailing and rocking as the fireman plucked her precious son out of her hands. I remember standing in the narrow hallway upstairs as the fireman was giving Danny mouth-to-mouth resuscitation as he flew down the stairs towards the ambulance. I remember desperately shaking Aunt Edna, screaming for her to wake up because Danny was dead, and then it was over. The priest was in our kitchen. He was actually comforting my mother with words like, "You have so many children, Connie. These things happen." I remember wanting to attack the man and rip his collar off, stomp on it and on him! The rest is a blur. I needed to retreat back to my blank state for just a short while.

We were allowed to go to Danny's funeral, at least the eldest ones. I'm not certain I believe it was the right call from our parents. You never forget a baby in a casket, especially when you are a mere child yourself.

So much white. White coffin, white flowers, white baby face with a white beautiful gown. So many clear tears flowing from men, women, and children. It was tragic. Our second sibling to die in a year's time would be the nail that sealed my mother's coffin... She may have been alive, but she resembled a walking zombie more than a mother the minute the tiny ghostly box was laid into the ground.

I didn't really know what a zombie was at age 9. I had not been privy to the film noir zombies of the fifties. What I did have was a mother walking around without the tattered clothing, outstretched arms, and lopsided walk. The pale complexion was shared by both, and of course, the absence of any emotion. This is what we were all left with after Danny's death.

Mom was stuck on the first stage of grieving: denial. My first indication of this was when I was asked to get Danny's bottle warmed up on the stove. She had the pan of water ready for immersion. As she approached with one of the younger siblings' baby doll in her arms, I instinctively knew our mother had become a stranger. The monster of grief had stolen our mother quickly. I tried to argue with her, softly mention that Danny was gone, but she would have none of it.

I did as I was told for several weeks, watching as she sat rocking and pretending to feed the plastic baby in blue. After Aunt Edna told Dad, the feedings stopped. Baby Danny was buried once again. This time under the piles of others in the upstairs toy box. The woman was now part of the walking dead, never to return to the land of the living for long.

Why couldn't they just let her pretend? What harm would it have done? Maybe some grief counseling would have been helpful, but then again, that's not the O'Donnell way.

The gin was now being delivered regularly by neighbors and taxi cab drivers. It was an old crutch with a proven record and a high proof to get Connie through the days.

Number three in the stages of grief was dancing into Mom's mind. The bargaining had begun... "Dear Lord, please give me another baby." Yvette was born only 15 months later in the summer month of June 1968. Mom's light returned, if only for a short while.

CHAPTER 34

Current of Chaos

I feel akin to Kya in *Where the Crawdads Sing*. Instead of living in the depths of the North Carolina marsh, I'm blanketed in the city of disfunction. It surrounds me. The shame of being who you are is mind-altering once the others lift your eyes to the new reflection... Now you see yourself in a completely different light. It's not really a light after all. It's a dark weight that will take a lot of strength, help, and miracles to be lifted, so you can finally become and see your authentic self—your true you staring back at your reflection.

The differences between Kya and me are obvious. Loneliness and abandonment were her weights. Mine were the complete opposite. Way too many people and vultures were holding me down, demanding my silence. She rose above, always in tune with her free spirit and her talents. I'm forever searching to become that magical phoenix rising from the ashes to become my true self. The younger you are when the pounds attach themselves, the harder it will be to set yourself free.

The ever-present current of chaos began, then loomed overhead on Sixth Street. It was soon creeping greedily forward four blocks away, hovering like an alien spacecraft over the 1009, and over the ten of us.

ABOVE THE BAR...

CHAPTER 35

Above the Bar

Aunt Edna was already living in the front apartment when Dad had the ill-omened idea to move the rest of us above the tavern.

We were excited about the move. It was a larger place with two bathrooms and six bedrooms. It was actually two apartments that we converted into one large living quarters. A brother duo named the Colby brothers were fixing things up in a mad rush. For some reason, our parents were in a hurry to make the four-block trek over to Tenth and Market.

Living above the tavern had its multi-functional benefits for all. Dad and Aunt Edna (our cook) had a one-minute daily commute down the back stairs to work. The children were happy to have pop and candy nearby for once, not to mention all the food we wanted from the kitchen for ourselves and friends. At first, it was a bit strange. None of us had been in the tavern much.

Watching Dad behind the bar was mesmerizing. He acted like a completely different person when on duty.

Our Dr.-Jekyll-and-Mr.-Hyde father began his transformation the second he ducked under the bar and headed for the back stairs for the remainder of his stay. The Hyde in him would come out if provoked or disturbed in any way. He was upstairs for only a few reasons... food, sleep, and control.

Mom was saving a bit of cash. No more taxi cab or neighbor fees, leaving her black patent leather purse for her medicine. She had all she needed right below her in quantities of mad proportions.

The nine of us were oblivious to the dangers lurking ahead. I think Dad and Edna were fully aware that things would never be the same, but they were unable and unwilling to change the course for the better.

As I was portraying a happy fifth-grader in 1968, my favorite *Barbra Streisand* was belting out Fanny Brice songs on film along with Omar Sharif. We were all great actors. The biggest difference is that they were getting paid, and they could sing. I had neither of these attributes in September or beyond. My acting career would take monumental indulgences with well-rehearsed lines from this age forward. I was a quick study. My peace and survival demanded nothing less.

Once my eyes were opened wide to the monster of alcoholism, the theatrical curtain fell. It was a hard thud and continued to rise and fall for the next several years. Like Barbra and myself, "A Star Was Born."

Theresa was the first to whisper the word "alcoholic" my way. I had no idea what she was saying. You might be thinking, "Denise should have known by now what an alcoholic was." You would have been wrong. So now the gin was out of the bottle. Theresa and then Aunt Edna explained the dreaded details of what both our parents had become. The shame was now present within my mind, body, and soul. The grand drape was rising... Act 1.

I was like an understudy, soaking up all around me. The lights were blinding and the emotions were overwhelming. Every minute of every day was exhausting as I used my mind to block out what my life was saying. I wished my life would just shut up.

The "other" activities were being given up the minute we moved above the bar, and we were already lacking in most of them. The housework, laundry, interaction, kindness, awareness, and caring were quickly being replaced by the gin. Now that my eyes were open, I had become Sherlock Holmes. "The Art of Deduction" was teaching me more than I could have ever imagined. My mother's drinking was on my mind constantly. I was putting my newly learned critical thinking skills to the test... But the test was really hard. I failed. If only I had the Internet back then, I would have learned quickly I was about to flunk any and every test I could dream up to help my mother.

Mom was my main concern, and my source of embarrassment. Dad, I was not so worried about. In a few short months of living "upstairs," the filth was creeping in on all sides. When the mom stops cleaning, it's to be expected, especially when over ten bodies live inside. Theresa tried desperately to keep the apartments clean. She finally gave up. I could see what was happening. I was disgusted, but not enough to follow in Theresa's footsteps. It was not my job to clean up after everyone. I decided to hole myself up in my room, keep it clean, do my own laundry, and count the days until I could escape.

The cigarette smoke was my biggest source of hatred and humiliation. I detested everything about their Salems. I was living in a plume of chemicals that could destroy my lungs every waking second. It's no wonder I developed asthma around the age of 15.

The little ones were dirty, the cockroaches were endless, the noise level was deafening, and yet we carried on. I became a hermit in my clean, red bedroom, trying thoroughly to never speak to my mother again.

Mom was still cooking, but not as much. We could run downstairs for all our nourishment if needed until Edna closed the kitchen. We were all driving Aunt Edna crazy I'm sure. The atmosphere would soon be the deciding force to drive our beloved second mother away; off to New Mexico she would run, never looking back. Her departure was soon after LaShawn and Stevie joined our motley crew.

CHAPTER 36

The Fargo

Nothing much was happening over at St. Mary's. We had a longer commute that became an issue only in the winter months. Fourth grade brought me a lay teacher, Mrs. Hodek. We met her while sitting in the church pews on our first day of fourth grade. She sashayed down the aisle in her turquoise miniskirt with matching shoes, hair down in waves of brown. She was a sight at our humble little Catholic school. I was not her favorite, it was plain to see, but she was nice enough.

The popular girls were getting her attention, Joanie and Meegan were the "it" girls. Meegan's father, Dr. Feeney, had delivered most of Connie's children. Mom says we built the pillars on their mansion, possibly even a bedroom or two. Meegan had long braids that were always in double golden unison trailing down her back. Joanie's father was a woodworker; he owned his own shop. Joanie had beautiful green eyes that set her apart from most others, especially alongside her lovely olive complexion. Meegan and Joanie both had three sisters each, a good number if you weren't the O'Donnells. They had been the popular girls since I became aware of them back in my second year of first grade. All I cared about was being their friend.

Peer pressure had set in. I would wait another two seasons before they sent a verbal invitation for friendship my way.

Theresa and I had found a new exciting activity, roller skating. It was heavenly. Wheels, music, boys, and an escape from the ordinary masses. The place was on the east side of DeKalb. The Fargo was the name and the music was the game. The old theater was perfect for the buzzing pre-teens. "Midnight Confessions," "Spooky," and "Born to Be Wild" were a few of our favorites. We couldn't get enough of the place! It wasn't hip enough for Meegan and Joanie. I had no idea what they were doing on Saturdays, and for once I didn't care.

The lowlifes in DeKalb were called hillbillies. I guess we fit that bill. Most of the 'billies were speed skating around with me and Theresa in grand style each and every weekend. Our prize skates were gifts from Aunt Edna right before we moved to the 1009. We really thought we were something, sporting our crisp white skates adorned with pink and blue pom-poms front and center. Our speed was paying off. We raced around in circles for hours, skating to the music and feeling free. And then it happened.

I was working with Aunt Edna in the kitchen when Dad got the call from the Fargo. Theresa was helping a little girl into the bathroom when someone on the other side of the big wood swinging door pushed the opposite way. Theresa's pinky finger was in the door, and now the first knuckle was on the floor! Dad flew out the door, grabbing a patron on the other side to tend bar while he was rushing to his eldest girl.

Unfortunately, the top part of her finger could not be attached. The doctor did a fairly decent job of sewing her up. To this day, her pinky is curved under with a new crude nail to match. Most folks don't notice her damaged finger, but then again, she's become a magician at hiding it.

CHAPTER 37

Teacher's Pet/Notre Dame

A s I sat in the classroom in fifth grade, I once again could hear the class in unison calling my name. This time, it was music to my ears. "Denise is a teacher's pet." I never tired of hearing that song. Mr. Maxim made it obvious he not only could tolerate me, but I was his favorite. I never questioned why. It was a newly found pleasure, one that I was not messing with any time soon.

The "in" crowd was seemingly inching closer to nice, which was completely throwing me off my game. It was enough for me to wonder, but not enough to lose sleep over. I had enough reasons for that.

Theresa was already over at the all-girls Catholic School of Notre Dame. I would follow her shortly. St. Mary's was becoming the land of the O'Donnells. Most of the inmates I was living with and a few cousins were thrown in the yard for good measure.

Behaving for me was never a problem. I was still scared to death of the penguins and the poppers. Theresa was not afraid of anyone. When she was at St. Mary's, she tormented the nuns continuously. The Notre Dame nuns were possibly meaner than the few Theresa left behind. She was in constant trouble with all the faculty. I wasn't looking forward to joining her on a daily basis. I had just gotten rid of her!

While Mom's personality was drastically changing, the kids were coming into their own. You may be wondering what we all looked like. Pretty much like one another and like Dad. We had no real concept of beauty or refinement. We were still much too young for all that nonsense. Mom used to say the blonds looked alike; that would be me, Layne, Tina, and Yvette. It's strange to think any of us were ever anything but brunette. All of us but Tina have the famous Irish turned-up nose, with small eyes to match. Yvette and Michele have the thin upper lip while the remaining eight have Dad's well-defined mouth.

I personally think all us girls have a manly appearance, strong features like Mom and Dad. In the mix of the ten, we have four blue-eyed children: Layne, Tina, Larry, and Stevie. Theresa, Denise, Michele, Sheila, and Yvette were lucky enough to inherit the Emerald Isle green. Lisa had deep brown beauties until recently a wee bit of the green has found its way in. We pretty much all resembled our father; even we could see it! Mom was a pretty gal with pretty green eyes and a perfect figure. Sheila wins the contest with the best figure and height in the line-up of girls.

In the upcoming years, we would hear others comment on our so-called good looks. Remember, we never heard either of our parents agree to this line of thinking, not once. They were our mirrors, and those mirrors were too fuzzy for the reflection of compliments or love.

We've discussed Theresa's personality, and by now you must be aware of mine. Michele was the constant question-asker. She was always grinning and asking silly questions. She drove Aunt Edna mad! Sheila was bossy, but sweet. Larry was mean and violent. Lisa was super quiet, always staring and afraid. Layne was the happiest, not a worry from her. Tina was quick, playful, and happy like Layne. Yvette was sweet, cute, and a joy. Steven was a doll. He had the shiniest hair and piercing blue eyes to match his sunny personality.

Larry caused most of the sibling fighting, while Theresa made certain there was madness among us daily. I believe, no, I know, my personality was altered once we moved above the tavern. Shame, fear, and hopelessness had thrown me into an angry pit of meanness. More than anything, I was just plain mad! The madness would continue until I left home. I was praying it would be sooner rather than later.

Right before the move over to the 1009, we were all ordered to sit around the kitchen table. Dad had an announcement to make. We knew it wasn't about another baby on the way; that was always a given. So there we sat, wondering what the news was going to be. I'm not sure why Dad was there at all. Mom was the one that blurted out the news, "Your father has joined the country club." The blank stares from the eldest that understood what a country club was were not responding accordingly, so Mom said it again. "It's the country club, members only. Your dad will be able to golf whenever he wants. You can go swimming at a private pool and dine at the clubhouse."

It was rare to see Mom this animated. Dad, as usual, was a statue. We asked a few questions, mainly about the pool. We should have been asking questions about why Dad really wanted to join the country club, but remember, we didn't know what a bookie was back then. The elite residents of DeKalb were aware of Dad's talents. They could now place a multitude of bets while hitting, sipping, and dining in the comfort of their precious establishment. It was way classier than slumming over at the 1009. Most of the wealthy of DeKalb would never have crossed the threshold of Dick's. It was definitely on the wrong side of the tracks.

Our pedaling was only a few blocks longer as we passed directly by Hopkins Park for the new, smaller watering hole. We jumped right in with the privileged few, many of which we knew personally, but we always felt we didn't belong. The stares from the others made certain we understood.

CHAPTER 38

Is She a Witch?/Dad's Tirades

The electricity of chaos was monumental, but the more obvious change was our mother's appearance. She transformed quickly and drastically. Looking back, it's easy now to give a name to why we watched our mother shrinking—she was anorexic. It was a new word and a new disorder for us to learn. It has followed a few of us throughout the years, still rearing its ugly head to the present day.

Remember, I was adept at hiding from Mom. I tried very hard to ignore her at all costs, but even I could see her downward slide away from a beauty queen. Never needing to lose weight in her life, the pounds fell off at lightning speed, causing her face to cave in, which gave her an eerie witch-like appearance. Mom was very pale with a prominent nose. When the weight came off, she became grotesquely tiny with nearly a hunchback appearance. Her straight ebony locks that she used to be so proud of were no longer her friend.

She was an extremely vain woman, but when disorders take over, one cannot really see the truth. She had a lighted, swinging make-up mirror that sat at our kitchen table for years. There she would apply her pancake foundation, drawn-on eyebrows, and bright red lipstick. It was always red! I never could understand how she could not see how she looked. It was obvious to everyone and only added to my dread of embarrassment that she was my mother.

While in seventh grade, our young hip bus driver asked if I knew the lady above the bar. I was surprised he was speaking to me at all. I of course said yes. He then asked, "Is she really a witch? Everyone tells me she's a witch." My only saving grace (this time) was, I was the last stop with nobody else in earshot of his question. My immediate thoughts were, "Doesn't he know she's my mother? He watches me go up the stairs above the bar daily. What an idiot." I did refrain from calling him a moron, but as I was jumping down the bus steps I did tell him, "No, she's not a witch and she's my mother." This was just one more reason to stay in my room and pray my mother would never go out in public again!

✞ ✞ ✞

Our father did not suddenly wake up one day as a dung beetle, resembling Gregor Samsa in the allegory of "The Metamorphosis," but there was a drastic personality shift in the man of the house as well. We were around Dad much more now, especially in the non-golfing months here in Northern Illinois. Dad was either downstairs working, upstairs eating, or most importantly watching his sports with a bit of sleeping in between. When Dad left the building, it was for one of three reasons: poker, drinking, and running the book.

Dad sometimes had to do his own running. He needed to collect his winnings. Sister Michele tells of being with Dad one winter evening as he ran all over the county stopping from bar to bar and house to house... running in for only minutes only to emerge empty-handed. She had no idea what he was doing or why she was a captive witness to the madness. Dad's shorty boots were the reason Michele didn't notice the mounds of cash he was retrieving. The rolled-up bills were tucked into his boots, only to be seen on his dresser the next morning as we took our lunch money. We were used to the mounds of money in sight, but not to the tirades Dad put us through once we moved above the bar.

We have finally pieced his episodes together. They most likely began with too much hard liquor, losing at poker, and possibly losing or betting against the book. Dad would come home late, barely able to stand, slurring and hunting, hunting for a child. Any of his offspring would do. Luckily for us, he took turns.

Once, I was in my room on the phone, talking to my friend Joanie. Dad flies in my room, yelling and grabbing at my princess streamline. Poor Joanie. He began to berate her for talking to me on the phone. He was screaming and mumbling. I'm certain she didn't understand much that was coming from his liquor-induced speech. I was desperately trying to grab the phone away from him with no luck. He finally threw the phone across the room, and now it was my turn.

On and on the tirade went, usually about my failure as a daughter, a student, and just a human in general. There was no getting away from him. We would just sit and cringe, praying there would be no physical injuries this time. We all would rush to our rooms when he returned home after his night of drink and losses. We learned in a nano-second when to hide, but as I stated before, the hiding places were non-existent—we were always found.

The worst of the tirades was directed at little brother Larry. It was still daylight when we heard the screams from the back porch as Dad began beating our only brother. It was without a doubt the most savage belting any of us had ever witnessed. It seemed to go on and on forever. I have always wondered why Larry didn't run down the back steps to get away from our monster of a father. I couldn't believe how long Dad was whipping him. Of course, Mom was doing nothing. Sitting in the kitchen, smoking, drinking her martini, looking at her reflection in her magnifying mirror. It was pitiful. This time, I had to run in my room and hide in my closet with my hands mushed on my ears while I sang a "la, la, la" stupid tune to drown out the screams and sounds of the leather belt upon Larry's young body.

Usually the beatings were never talked about again, back to normal the minute the thrashing was halted. It was the summer, so no teachers or authorities were notified. After this nightmare of torture, Theresa, Michele, Sheila, and I put a stop to any more physical forms of punishment from Dad. We waited, and then, as a foursome, we ventured downstairs late one night and convinced Dad to stop the madness. We had learned from the best. Bribery was a hard pill to swallow for the master puppeteer. I'm wondering why we didn't confront him earlier. I guess the fear got in the way.

In the throngs of a shamble we called life, we were all expected to go to school, act normal, and learn. The teachers, including nuns and priests, were not very bright when it came to diagnosing abused children, at least not the ones gazing our way. We did have the one reprieve with

Michele's black eye incident, but once we were above the bar, things started back up.

I suppose the black-and-white staff at St. Mary's had enough headaches making certain their men in cloth stayed out of the limelight and the local papers. Time would catch a priest, but it would be generations before the abuses caught up with the abusers in our humble little town of DeKalb.

Late one night as I was retrieving my laundry, I spotted Father Damien scurrying out our back door. Was that really our priest in our house? He moved with ease, quietly, almost bat-like as he flew down our backstairs to his lair. Was I dreaming? Had I been watching *Dark Shadows* too many years? Was my reality of make-believe and sound mind playing tricks on me?

The next morning when I was forced to speak with Mom, she just looked the other way and told me "Don't worry about it." I would learn decades later Michele was ordered the same words of caution by both Mom and Dad.

Brother Larry was an altar boy. When not at the pulpit, he was sleeping near the back door, upstairs—whether or not he was safe and sound would be the question. Was Larry a member of the young boys hurt by this deviant beast? Like Dad at the Falcons Club, this priest was free to roam the parish. Hunting for adolescents would prove to be as easy as running the "book." Both men had their disgusting addictions, possibly leading them both straight down the road to perdition.

CHAPTER 39

Demoralization

We never knew what we would find when we walked in the door after school. One day I found Mom passed out in the middle of the kitchen in a lawn chair. The broiler under the stove was on fire. After throwing sugar on the flames, I began screaming to wake her up. She was not happy. The Valium may have had something to do with the newfound afternoon slumber she was getting. What crazy doctor prescribes a well-known alcoholic mother of ten with diazepam? I realize Valium can be given to treat alcoholism, but that is not why Mom is throwing them back. She needed a high, more than the gin was supplying.

What on Earth was Dad thinking? Seriously, how could he not care what was happening all around him? We were all getting more verbal, more angry, and more scared for the little ones' lives. This was becoming dangerous. There would be countless accidents between siblings, attacks from siblings, siblings getting stuck in trees, falling down manholes, getting run over, slashing arms open, and scars from Larry attacks. Yvette was lost for four hours at age 4. Once, Stevie was found hanging outside the window. Sheila made certain safety issues were in place. Nails were finally used to lock down the upstairs back porch windows. Daily madness of unsurpassed proportions were our constant shadows, and they were all dark.

Sixth grade brought a large shadow into place, with my new and last teacher at St. Mary's in full view. Sister Mary Rose Marie. Short and stocky, never a smile crossed her lips. As she called on me mid-year to the chalkboard, I was shaking as I made my way through the aisle. It was a dreaded math question. I hated math. When I finally had to admit I didn't know the answer, she went crazy! She grabbed me by my shoulders and began shaking me violently back and forth, all the while screaming at me to take my awful sweater off as she berated me with the accusations of ignorance, bad hygiene, and demoralization. When she was finally done, my green sweater was lying on the floor in a heap. The entire class was in shock. Even for a nun, this was bizarre behavior! I was ordered to sit down. I did as I was told. Humiliation was monumental as the minutes went by until I could rush home. It was worse than Mrs. Newmann in her heyday; it really was. My parents were not concerned. They said I must have had it coming. That was always their answer for me.

A few weeks later, there was a big hygiene lesson in the same classroom. As I sat listening, I knew without fail that the lesson was directed at me—well, mainly me. The profuse sweating and lack of deodorant was still a realization, not to mention the infrequent bathing. The immersion course was a success! First of all, I went home screaming at my mother. This was all her fault. Why hadn't she taught us to be clean! Why no deodorant? Couldn't any of the adults smell my body odor? Maybe the cigarettes clouded their sense of smell. I was beyond crazy!

From that day forward, I bathed every single day, scrubbing myself almost raw. I had shiny hair, clean porcelain skin, and deodorant. I felt wonderful. The prayers of the parish faculty had been answered. The only ailment sticking around was the sweating. It would take me decades to learn that this was an actual disorder called hyperhidrosis. It can be hereditary, which is one horrible condition that I borrowed from my father and passed on to my children. It's almost under control these days, but every once in a while it rears its ugly, sweaty head my way.

✝   ✝   ✝

We all lived in fear of Yvette's seizures. It's quite frightening to witness an infant and then toddler shaking with eyes rolling at any given moment. Her episodes usually began with a thump on the head, so we followed her around trying to keep this from happening. Many times, we would witness Dad flying up the back stairs to help with number nine and her disorder. We had no clue at the time that epilepsy was a direct result of the gin. It would take another anomaly for me to figure out the meaning of birth defects brought on by the evils of alcohol.

I was 13 the year LaShawn was born. Yes, we had another sister. We were pretty shocked when she was born. We thought maybe the babies were going to stop. I was in seventh grade over at the all-girls Catholic school of Notre Dame. Theresa and I arrived off the bus and wondered where Mom was... Something was very, very wrong. Dad was behind the bar as usual. He seemed odd. We asked where Mom was, but he wouldn't answer. We found Aunt Edna in the backroom behind the tavern kitchen. She was crying. We instinctively thought Mom had died. Someone had better start talking. Theresa and I were hysterical. It would only be a matter of time before the others were upon us...

We were a bit calmed down when we finally heard Mom was alive. Our next question was, "Did she have the baby?"

Edna's crying became louder as she tried to speak. "Yes, she had the baby. It's a girl, but she's deformed."

Theresa and I were staring and frowning, "What are you saying? What does 'deformed' mean?"

"Her name is LaShawn and she has legs like a mermaid."

We were in disbelief and shocked by this news. We were having a difficult time understanding or believing our Aunt. Speaking to Dad was not allowed. I think we told Michele and Sheila the horrid news and one by one the others became aware. At least those who could understand. We walked around in a daze. Once again, tragedy had followed Mom to the birthing room and beyond.

The medical term for a "mermaid" baby is "sirenomelia." To this day, I've never seen a photo of a baby like LaShawn. I'm wishing now I hadn't looked it up. It's a sad and disturbing anomaly, taking on a science fiction characteristic, ghastly and unforgettable. Luckily our parents chose to cover our precious sister while she lay in her white casket. She resembled an angel, so much like Mary and Danny before her. Her face was all we needed to see. Our love was our only emotion for her tiny soul.

LaShawn lived a bit over a month—born on April 21, 1970, and passed on May 25 of the same year. She was scheduled for surgery in Chicago, but never made the journey from DeKalb. She died the day before the operation was to begin.

I was still in my red hideout, emerging for food, laundry, and my daily bath. We didn't talk about LaShawn much. There was no reason to. Mom and Dad both were becoming adept at burying their children. I'm sure our cousin John Ronan would have preferred a sabbatical when it came to greeting us at his mortuary. When Dad's voice was recognized over the phone, I'm guessing John wanted to cry.

The good news was, LaShawn was the last of the O'Donnell children to grace his establishment, but not the last of the family to lie in his back room awaiting the service up front. Paying for funerals could not have been easy for Richard and Connie. I always wondered if they had any help.

Steven was born in the summer month of June 1971. He would be the last. The baby brigade had ended. When Mom came home from the hospital, Steven was handed to Michele as she waited outside the bar. Connie walked up the concrete steps, never skipping a beat. Her gin, Salems, and barstool were waiting. The still-handsome bartender was adding her precious olive as she slid into her seat. All was well for the adults once again.

✟ ✟ ✟

Two boys had flashlights, and they had my sister Theresa. Luckily I was not asked if I wanted a ride while exiting Hopkins Park with the crazy one. She got in their back seat, leaving me to walk home in the dusk alone. This is one time I wish she would have just stayed with me. We cannot go back in time, no matter how tragic the memories have become.

As she finished this horror story with me, she also shared an incident that happened with a neighbor girl from across the street. This particular type of abuse even shocked Theresa. Her courage and outcries would stay a secret until I began my book. She did inform our parents about the flashlight attack immediately, but true to form, they told her never to mention it again.

She barely knew the older boys. One was a very distant cousin, and the reason she thought nothing of getting a ride back to the 1009. She was in her mid-teens. These things were not talked about. They drove somewhere safe and took turns holding her down while the other used their flashlights as telescopes into her body. She said she wasn't screaming or thrashing like I did with my first attacker. She says she went into shock. I sometimes wish I didn't know this story. It's difficult to get the image out of your head.

I've only run into the "cousin" once since hearing this account, and it was all I could do but attack him myself. He still lives in DeKalb. He is a member of our country club, where I witnessed him laughing at the bar with a lovely drink in his hand, carefree and unaware I knew the secret he shared with my older sister. My prayers were not answered it seems. I was sharing an address with others in the same sorted club as myself. The abused children's club was growing. The number on the building was 1009.

CHAPTER 40

Stunned

My sweater snatcher, Sister Mary Rose Marie, must have had a conscience after all. No doubt it was hiding up in her pointy headdress. One random day, she cornered me in the hallway alone. My first thought was, "Hang on to your sweater, Denise." Luckily, she was not reaching for my shoulders for a shaking. What she said next has stuck with me and brought me to wonder time and time again over my sixty-two years. The popular girls had finally invited me ever so slowly into the circle of fame. I was now the newest member of their small club.

My teacher had noticed this new turn of events. She was concerned. "Denise, do not become their friend. Stay away from them. They are trouble." Stunned in the hallway for many reasons, the first being a nun is actually speaking to me. Maybe she's trying to help me in some bizarre way… I was having none of it. I've been waiting for six years to become part of the in-crowd. I just barely was inducted into the circle. I was not breaking the chain now.

No nun, priest, or God himself could convince me to turn my back on Meegan and Joanie. Not now, not ever.

We traded in our blues for greens and grays. Yet another ugly, itchy wool ensemble announcing our place of education was on the horizon. Theresa and I were now catching the big bus over at St. Mary's parking lot for our fifteen-minute journey to Notre Dame. At the time, it was state of the art. A beautiful campus with the nuns' residence sharing the property next door. We had a trampoline, an in-ground pool, a huge gymnasium, and best of all, no stupid boys were allowed!

I had one full year at the facility. It closed due to lack of funding. After getting slapped across the face by yet another nun, I can admit, I was ready for a change of scenery. Theresa actually made me proud during a pep assembly one afternoon while at Notre Dame. She was awarded the most-improved student of the year.

Theresa had spent an entire school year living with a DeKalb policeman and his schoolteacher wife. Bob and Kathy took her in on the pleading and advice from the social workers and mental health experts over at Ben Gordon. I was very jealous. She had a clean home and her own beautiful bedroom. She had adults that talked to her, taught her, and loved her—no fair! I guess if you are bad enough, good things will come to you. At least, that was my thinking back then.

Our entire family became friends with Bob and Kathy. They were exceptional people. Bob and Theresa still keep in touch to this day. The only reason Theresa came home was to help when Steven was born. She was afraid Mom was unable to raise him. She was correct. I was now off to North Junior High, while Theresa was headed to our DeKalb High School. Things were starting to look up.

Meegan was being sent to the University private school called "Lab." She lived blocks from North Junior High. As kids, we couldn't understand why her parents would make her go to a private school when the free public school was down the street. Dr. Feeney wasn't one to change his mind easily, so Joanie and I were forced to visit Meegan on the weekends only. There were a handful of us Catholic students mixing in with many strangers from around town. I had no idea DeKalb had so many people I never heard of, and many non-Catholics. Amazing!

Theresa was gifted with a 1959 Desoto from Dad. It was a sight. Push-button dash, ugly gray with a backseat the size of a mansion sofa. It was a riot! For some odd reason, my older sister also decided to be my friend. She would bring a few of the Lab boys over to North for a pleasure cruise almost daily. Like a flash through the circle wraparound she would fly. I was always waiting with a smile for Theresa and the boys!

Sometimes Meegan would be in tow. She was the ringleader over at Lab, introducing me to the cool crowd never got old. My popularity was growing. For some reason, the boys were almost excited to be around me. The oddities just kept coming. It was probably the fun car rides, the music, and the laughter. It had nothing to do with me. Theresa was our chauffeur, supplying all of us with endless joy for many an afternoon special.

I became friends easily and happily with many. We played flag football, went to the Northern games, spent countless hours in downtown DeKalb, and played softball all summer long. We swam and listened to music like it was 1999! My brain was on fire with the happiness of being popular. "All I wanted to do was have some fun." Sheryl Crow would have been proud!

Upstairs, everyone was getting older. That meant more bodies above the bar. Most of us were very social extroverts. We wanted friends desperately. Yes, we were embarrassed because of the conditions, probably me more than any.

Theresa was back; she was cleaning again while screaming at Mom about the house and the kids. All the extra children made me angry. They were very loud and for whatever reason they stayed up day and night, hardly sleeping at all. The summer months were the worst, so I stayed busy in my room. I babysat, I listened to music on my new stereo, I talked on my private phone, and I kept my door shut at all costs.

The massive fish fries we served every Friday had become famous. We had breaded catfish, deep-fried perch, scallops, awesome thick French fries with homemade coleslaw and a roll. Mom was the only in-house waitress, something she could handle under the influence easily. Her days at the tap were paying off. She saved her tips all year for our Christmas gifts. She was absolutely a fan of Christmas.

Michele and I were the duo sisters in the kitchen. We would take turns helping Aunt Edna and Dorothy until the take-outs had ended and the patrons were out the door. It was a sad, sad day when Dad decided to close the kitchen. The factory workers were upset—no more quick lunches, now only shots served at noon. The Wednesday night specials also ceased, but the fish dinners were always the favorite, missed by all over at the 1009.

One Friday afternoon, during Christmas break, Michele decided she wanted a raise. It seemed like thirty cents per hour was not her idea of a fair wage. One of the regulars overheard her asking Dad for a raise to no avail. The next thing Dad knew the factory workers were all coming in on their lunch hour laughing and giving Dad all kinds of hell calling him a tightwad and accusing him of practicing unfair child labor laws. He had absolutely no idea what they were all talking about until he noticed his third-born daughter with picket in hand for all the ruffians to see. Immediately he ducked under the bar, ran out, and snatched Michele back inside to resume her shift with a fifteen-cent per hour raise. The picket sign was destroyed at the same moment Michele's smile was applied to her face. She knew she had won at least this round. It was one of Dad's tall tales he would tell from behind the bar for years to come, the exception being that this tall tale was actually true.

✞   ✞   ✞

When not eating at our own establishment, we would head towards the country club for a nice dinner out. We usually didn't have much notice. Mom or Dad would arrive in the back end announcing a wardrobe change. Time was wasting! After a few embarrassing moments at the club with Michele, she was alienated from the dining room. We then had to change in secret. Sometimes she knew what we were doing and would rush out the door desperately trying to squeeze in the car. Once, she actually chased us down the street. I have to admit, we understood why the parents didn't want her at the club. She even embarrassed us. Michele had always been obsessed with food and money. We have no idea why. She would ask the waitress all kinds of questions. She would argue with Dad over ordering choices, and a time or two, she licked her plate. These are not the attributes to possess for a smooth dining experience with Mom and Dad. They will get you kicked out of the club.

I wanted to feel like a normal family. A night on the town was special for our disfunctional crew. The problem was being seen in public with Mom. The others at the table didn't seem to care. They had no idea the compromise I was making to feel normal and wanted.

Grandpa O'Donnell passed away in 1969. It was a massive heart attack. Grandma Lou would follow him six years later. Cancer took her slowly. We were still seeing our cousins about once a year at O'Donnell picnics over at Aunt Charlene's or Aunt Joan's. The pie-eating contest had gone out of style, unfortunately. I always came in second behind Cousin Annette. We loved seeing our big extended family. We only wished it could have been more often.

Mom's parents had moved to New Mexico. They had had enough of the cold Missouri winters and the constant threat of tornados. Trailers and tornados do not go hand in hand. Uncle Billy and family were all set up in the Land of Enchantment when they arrived. The next George to follow would be none other than our very own Aunt Edna.

The shocking announcement was chilling. We were at a loss for words. As the air was leaving our lungs, we finally had a release of enlightenment. Of course she was leaving. Who would want to stay here if they didn't have to? We were waiting in the tavern when she exited the building. Shrills of crying children were the last sounds she heard as Kenny escorted her to O'Hare. Our savior was now on a mission of her own, saving herself and tending to her ailing parents. Aunt Edna would prove to be excellent at both.

I never asked Mom or Dad how they felt about her departure. I'm sure Mom felt abandoned and Dad had lost his infamous cook. The kitchen would be closed within a few short years. She was a tough cook to follow.

CHAPTER 41

Beer Snatching

Theresa had traded her boat in for a Trans Am sports car and had decided to quit high school. She was driving out to Hobbs, New Mexico, to join Mom's side of the family. Lucky for her, GTE had an office in the same small town as Aunt Edna. Theresa had secured a place to live. She became the top salesman month after month in her Main Street office. Theresa shared the same work ethic our father had. She was like a chameleon. Her customers never knew her any other way than professional.

I was the lone O'Donnell wolf in high school, waiting only one year for Michele and then Sheila to join our social club of learning.

My summer before high school, I was asked to do a terrible thing: steal from my father. New-found friend Maggie wanted beer. I was being tested. Tested by my peers and tested by God. My peers won out. I was a nervous wreck trying to figure out how to get the warm six-pack of Budweiser out of the back room and into a brown sack without my dad becoming alarmed.

Well, Friday nights were still super busy thanks to the multitude of Catholics waiting in line for their fish. My life of crime had begun. I walked the two-mile trek to Maggie's with my pajamas wrapped around the red cans, hoping a squad car could not recognize the shape I was clutching so tightly.

We sat on her beautiful deck off her classy home sharing the beers between us. It was disgusting. How on Earth was my father making a living selling this awful stuff! Later it occurred to me, he wasn't. Dad did make his living selling, but it wasn't cool liquids. It was the "book" he was selling, and he was doing great. But even the luck of the Irish can run out from time to time. Dad was living on borrowed time. His green clover started to fade. He had been warned.

By now there were three of us gracing the halls of the high school—the same halls our grandfather had swept as a janitor after his farming retirement. Little sister Michele had become a cheerleader and Sheila a dancing queen. I was very proud of them. They were both very good. They could stomp, scream, keep time to the music, and flip all over the gymnasium floor. I wasn't very proud at 11 p.m. on school nights when they continued this display of announcement from their shared bedroom! My understanding was we all needed sleep. I guess I was wrong.

I'm not certain what infuriated me more, the constant noise or the stealing of my clothes by my sisters and my sisters' friends. I was a clothes horse. I worked hard in the cornfields in the summer making sure I could afford the best. Michele and Sheila worked little and stole a lot. It was a constant reason for massive fights throughout the years. Michele actually got a padlock for her walk-in closet. There she kept my clothes at ransom for weeks on end until she felt like returning them... Unbelievable.

They learned from the best. I was known to take a few Bobbie Brooks outfits from Theresa before I became wealthy myself. One day, she beat me home for my quick change. She became her hysterical self in an instant. She completely demolished my bedroom. She threw my prized typewriter out the second-story window along with my new chenille curtains and bedspread.

Mom had surprised me with a suite redo on my 16th birthday. It was now all ruined. I could see the fabric on the ground as I drove up, lying in the snow with my typewriter face down upon my black and white presents from Mom. I felt sorrier for Mom than myself. It was a sad sight to behold. The crazy had not left the child. She was still a clear and present danger to any who crossed her. I never borrowed any of her clothes again. She still scared the crap out of me.

Normally I didn't have groups of friends rushing up to me as I walked into school. This would be one of two days in the upcoming year that would prove me wrong. This time I missed all the action over at the 1009. The action was above the bar, not below. I had spent the night with Kim the previous school night (I was helping her with her reading). As I pushed open the double side doors, the masses were in sight. Everyone was asking me questions all at the same time. "Did he try to get you? Did your dad have to fight him? Was he a teenager? Is your sister okay?"

Seriously, I had no idea what they were all talking about. I was safe down the street in Kim's room where men don't hide under beds. This only happens above the bar! Until Michele and Sheila confirmed this account minutes later, I was an unbeliever.

As Lisa and Layne were sleeping in the front room nearest the fluorescent Dick's 1009 sign, a man was lying in wait. Yes, he was under their bed. Layne thought she felt a breeze, but went back to sleep. She instantly knew the hand around her ankle was a reason to scream. The commotion commenced, kids jumping, parents running, a strange man in a foreign language pleading for his life. Dad did not speak Spanish, unless it was "cerveza." No beers were being served upstairs this night.

The police were called, the man was hauled away, but no formal charges were filed. He said he was drunk and lost his way, somehow ending up under our sister's bed, clutching her leg. It all was too embarrassing for me to tolerate, beyond humiliation, and yet another reason rising up to remind us all we were not normal. The entire town was becoming aware of this.

A few months later, the second round of news was plastered all over the front page of the DeKalb *Chronicle*. They were spreading the news, "Dick's 1009 has been shut down due to illegal gambling. John Richard O'Donnell has been fined $1,000 and ordered to close the doors of his establishment for ten days beginning immediately. The state liquor board had begun looking into the proprietor's unsavory behavior. A move may be imminent concerning Mr. O'Donnell's well-sought-after license in the near future."

There was an undercover police officer that befriended both my parents. He was in charge of the sting operation. Some think it was really an FBI takedown, but we may never know. The three of us once again were greeted at school with questions about the "Mafia."

"Is your dad in the Mafia? Did you see the FBI officers? Did you see them haul your father off? Was your mom there?"

We didn't know a thing. We didn't know until the ink was dry on the front page. We must have been at school when it happened, so why were we not told until the rest of the town was notified?

Mafia, really? Our dad is not Italian; he is Irish. The high school boys seemed excited, almost impressed, but personally I was mortified. This was worse than the man under the bed. It was personal. I needed to get out of this place. Time was on my side. The older I became, the closer I got to freedom. I was counting the days until my release of this nightmare I called life.

By now you understand the way our household worked. Of course we were not told anything. No sense in wasting words. Our children can hear about it like all the other people in DeKalb. The news!

I remember the undercover cop. He seemed very out of place, not a regular-looking barfly. I noticed that immediately. Later he apologized to Mom and Dad, saying he didn't really want to shut Dad down. He became a quick friend and then an even quicker enemy. I'm not sure of all the particulars concerning the gambling pool. It was illegal and Dad was caught red-handed. This was true, however, Dad was not arrested. He was only fined. And why did he keep his license?

Maybe the faded clover was soaking up some chlorophyll after all. Could it have come over from the Green Mill via I-88? It does make one wonder, doesn't it? Dad didn't seem concerned. When asked questions, he just rotated his ever-present toothpick around and looked the other way. The toothpick was his trademark, only replaced by cigarettes when needed. Richard was getting an instant, well-deserved, unpaid vacation, starting immediately.

CHAPTER 42

Graduation and Goodbyes

I was hiding in the bathroom most of the evening in my royal blue cap and gown. It was my high school graduation, and I was without parents or grandparents lighting my way towards higher education. Flashbulbs were pointed at groups of friends and families. The festivities were endless. I felt like a fool just standing near other proud parents as I said nothing when asked, "Where are your parents, Denise?" The bathroom was my hideout. No red bedroom here for escape.

Tami's parents were my favorites. They didn't ask me a thing. Betty and Gene knew us very well, even though we just met Tami, Susan, and brother David four years earlier. Sheila was very good friends with Susan. We would pass one another in the halls at each other's homes often. I kinda had a crush on Mr. Goral. He was the first to find my high school photo under his pillow one night. Wishing Gene was my father was a given. He was a good, solid man. Betty was my favorite mother, kind, clean, and nice. They treated us differently, maybe because they came in from

Dixon late in our lives, having no preconceived ideas about me, Sheila or our crazy family.

I found my father lying on the sofa when I returned. I was filled with rage, absolute rage. He told me he could not go to my graduation because it was a Friday night. There was no question of asking another bartender to take his shift. I was even willing to allow Mom to go, and she had slid further down the slide of strange by this time. Her appearance was becoming ghastly. They didn't show up for my Confirmation back in sixth grade either, even after I took all the weekly classes for months. Their refusal to go brought back memories of my first day in kindergarten. I instinctively knew when the embarrassment and fear set in together, staying put was my only option. This time I had no choice; I was graduating even if I did it alone.

I threw a fit. The screaming lasted a few minutes with Dad defending himself over and over again. He said he had just gotten off work and had just sat down when I entered in my cap and gown. I was the first child to graduate. I thought it was something to see. Once again my thinking wasn't matching the adults in the house. I was beyond hurt and embarrassed by their behavior. Mom was silent. She knew when to be quiet. Maybe she had her own hiding place somewhere. Good for her. We all needed a safe room for our sanity in this house.

✟ ✟ ✟

What do sloe gin, Mad Dog, vodka, peppermint schnapps, regular gin, and whiskey all have in common? Other than the fact they are all liquor, they were what was stolen out of the back storeroom by the second daughter in question. Remember, I was in high school for fun. It was never about learning.

If not for my first-period art teacher, I wouldn't have graduated. For some reason, she never marked me absent. Art, English, and Home Economics were my three favorite classes. I was forever making scarves on looms, writing, or cooking. These passions have followed me throughout my life, bringing many hours of pleasure, not to mention several careers.

I missed a lot of Mondays in school. I was usually mentally exhausted by Sunday night. Getting through two days above the bar wore me out.

Was I popular because I was likable, or was I likable because I had free access to booze? Or could it have been my Mustang? Dad kept telling me he was getting me a sports car. I wasn't too excited. I remember the DeSoto he gifted Theresa her freshman year. That memory crushed my hopes of driving anything cool.

Months went by and one day Dad called upstairs and told me to look out the back window. He had a surprise for me. It was black and white. It was a really awesome car... a 1967 Mustang in very good condition. I don't think I had ever run down the back stairs quicker in my life. Dad was behind the bar. With a slight grin on his face, he handed me the keys. "I paid the first payment. I'll pay your insurance; starting right now you will owe me $50 each month for your car. You better find a job."

A Colby brother had finally released his car to Dad. Paying off gambling debts had always proven excellent for my transportation over the years. I was now the owner of the coolest automobile of my life... I became a chauffeur immediately. The first place I drove was down to Ninth Street to pick up Joanie, Kim, and then Caroline. Joanie always thought it was hysterical that Dad gave me a car and then ordered me to find a job. I didn't care in the least. Working got me out of the smoke-filled house and away from the endless noise and filth upstairs.

By now, the smoke plume was becoming larger. The teens in the house had taken up smoking as well. I was beside myself with this new realization: I detested cigarettes! Tami and I were the only friends not puffing away constantly. I had rules against smoking in my car, but my rules fell on deaf ears. My saving grace was that the windows were down most of the time. The winter months were the worst.

Most of my good friends were headed off to college. Higher education was calling their names. College was never mentioned in our house. Not once did Mom or Dad ask me what I was planning for my future.

I spent my last summer bonding with my friends and rushing back and forth from Hopkins Park to the country club and then to the ballpark. It kept me happy and busy. My team was "Dick's 1009." I was one of two pitchers on the team. I was fairly good, but not great at hitting like Sheila. She was the home run queen. The problem with that was, she was our competition, just like Michele.

I was saying goodbye to a few past boyfriends as well. One was off to Utah, the other to the Naval Academy. They both hold a special place in my heart. Young love is amazing. I see them from time to time, usually making a fool of myself when they are near.

It was extremely difficult to say goodbye to Meegan. She had moved in with us for about six months. She brought a puppy home. Soon they were both out in the snow. I was called from the corner payphone near her mansion. Mom and Dad said it was fine to have Meegan become part of our family. She was already a favorite by all.

Meegan liked Mom. They would sit and smoke in the kitchen for hours. I would just shake my head at Meegan. I could never understand why she would want to chat with my mother! My sisters' friends were the same way. They really liked Mom. Dad would give Meegan his car, usually right after I asked and he told me no. It was a silly game Dad played, but we were on to his devious ways by then. It was nice to have an air-conditioned sedan every once in a while. Meegan didn't seem to care that she left an amazing, beautiful home for the lower social level of the upstairs. She was a true friend. I treasure our friendship greatly.

✟   ✟   ✟

While Paul Simon was singing "50 Ways to Leave Your Lover," I was contemplating fifty ways to leave DeKalb. I was stopped in my tracks by Dad one morning as I sat in my room. He needed a bartender. He had to be joking. He knew I detested everything about the 1009. He told me to get downstairs for my first day of training. I slammed my phone down. I was fuming with rage, but down the stairs I went. It was a sad day.

The arguing with Dad about how I hated the bar, the smoke, the clientele, and especially my barfly of a mother did no good. I was his only choice it seemed. Without these few hours of training, my eight total hours talking with my dad would have been reduced to four. I succumbed to helping him for three reasons: I needed a job, I wanted to be close to Dad, and I knew he needed my help. Turns out, I was a fairly good barkeep. I was fast and I kept the "till" full of money. I worked the 3:30 to 8:00 p.m. shift daily, no days off. Our bar was the only bar in town open on Sundays. We also had the coldest beer in town, thanks to an ancient cooler that kept on ticking.

I was a bit afraid we would get robbed again. I wasn't looking forward to a sawed-off shotgun in my face like the previous robbery several years back. No one was hurt. Dad was playing poker when the gunman came in. Little Joe the bartender didn't respond quickly enough to his demands, but soon decided he better comply. The patrons also lost their cash and jewelry.

I refused to make my mother's martinis, so she would just come back behind the bar and help herself. If Dad and I were both working side by side, he was her hero. No amount of talking to either of them about her diseases worked. She was free to stay the way she wanted, the way they both wanted. In a blurry daze with no cares ahead, numb to the realities surrounding them or the realities of their children. When I finally left, there were still eight more children at home. Things would only get worse.

CHAPTER 43

New Mexico

The country club's ladies' room, the floor, and Mom. These were the deciding factors that catapulted me to New Mexico. Theresa was home on vacation; I was soon to follow her back. New Mexico was going to inherit another Illinois transplant.

In between the appetizers and the main course, Theresa found Mom passed out under the stalls in the pink bathroom at the club. Luckily she was escorted (carried) out the side entrance with not many onlookers. It came in handy to have a wife weighing only 90 pounds when it was necessary to haul her over your shoulder.

An old lifeguard boyfriend asked me to drive out to Amarillo, Texas, with him. He was the answer to my prayers. Dad released me from the bar and as they say, the rest is history. Theresa and her first husband rescued me from Texas... Aunt Edna had a spare room. I was her new roommate. Grandma and Grandpa were happy to embrace another one of Connie's children. My Irish luck was finally kicking in. It sure took its time!

Mom cried like a baby when I told her I was leaving. She kept saying, "I'll never see you again." Dad gifted me with an extra $100 bill and a hug, followed by an "I love you." It seems one must leave the home before any sentiments are uttered by the parents. How very strange. I'm not complaining, just trying to understand the reasoning behind their oddities. A lifetime of thinking has brought little light to these questions.

THE
LOWER EIGHT

CHAPTER 44

The Lower Eight

A million shattered dreams were not on my mind when I left home. My dreams were just beginning. The advantages I possessed were an inquisitive mind, vivid memories, and the will to get through to the other side. My prayers were that the lower eight would forgive my departure and understand why.

They came into the game wounded, hurting, misguided, and afraid. Their demons came before, during, and hopefully not after. Only when you need love can you become so hurt. They loved us. They just didn't know the course for release... As I said before, "The pretending will destroy your life."

I used to pray that my time on this planet could have been different, altered. Not for dramatic purposes, but for self-preservation. But now I realize this was my destiny, my path. It was the path of the ten. We are who we were meant to become.

Embracing our past will set us free in ways unimaginable. Owning our past lives will be the answer to the freedom and the end of the illusion.

THE END.